Foreword

This Exam Preparation guide is intended for those preparing for the Cisco Certified Internetwork Expert for the Storage Networking Track Exam.

This book is **not** a replacement for completing a course. This is a study aid to assist those who have completed an accredited course and are preparing for the exam.

Do not underestimate the value of your own notes and study aids. The more you have, the more prepared you will be.

While it is not possible to pre-empt every question and content that may be asked in the CCIE-Storage Networking exam, this book covers the main concepts covered within the CCIE discipline.

Each process contains a summarized overview of key knowledge. These overviews are designed to help you to reference the knowledge gained through the course.

Due to licensing rights, we are unable to provide actual CCIE Exams. However, the study notes and sample exam questions in this book will allow you to more easily prepare for a CCIE exam.

Ivanka Menken
Executive Director
The Art of Service

Write a review to receive any *free* eBook from our Catalog - $99 Value!

If you recently bought this book, we would love to hear from you! Benefit from receiving a free eBook from our catalog at http://www.emereo.org/ if you write a review on Amazon (or the online store where you purchased this book) about your last purchase!

How does it work?

To post a review on Amazon, just log in to your account and click on the Create your own review button (under Customer Reviews) of the relevant product page. You can find examples of product reviews in Amazon. If you purchased from another online store, simply follow their procedures.

What happens when I submit my review?

Once you have submitted your review, send us an email at review@emereo.org with the link to your review, and the eBook you would like as our thank you from http://www.emereo.org/. Pick any book you like from the catalog, up to $99 RRP. You will receive an email with your eBook as download link. It is that simple!

Table of Contents

FOREWORD 1

TABLE OF CONTENTS 3

1 CISCO CERTIFIED INTERNETWORK EXPERT 9

2 EXAM SPECIFICS 10

2.1 EXAM PREREQUISITES 11

3 STORAGE NETWORK STANDARDS 12

3.1 FIBRE CHANNEL STANDARDS 12
3.1.1 Fibre Channel 12
3.1.2 Topologies 12
3.1.3 Fibre Channel Layers 13
3.1.4 Fibre Channel Ports 13
3.2 SCSI PROTOCOLS 14
3.2.1 SCSI Command 15
3.2.2 Logical Unit Number 16
3.2.3 SCSI Protocol Layers 16
3.3 iSCSI 17
3.3.1 SCSI Concepts 17
3.3.2 Internet Storage Name Service 18
3.4 INTERNET PROTOCOL 20
3.4.1 IPv4 Addressing 20
3.4.2 IPv6 22
3.4.3 Subnetting 24
3.4.4 Classless Interdomain Routing 27
3.4.5 Supernetting 28
3.4.6 Public and Private Addresses 29
3.4.7 Network Access Translation 30
3.4.8 Port Address Translation (PAT) 31
3.5 FIBRE CHANNEL AND IP 32
3.5.1 Fibre Channel over IP 32
3.5.2 Internet Fibre Channel Protocol 32
3.6 FICON 33

4 **DESIGNING AND IMPLEMENTING SANS** **35**
4.1 UNDERSTANDING THE CUSTOMER 35
4.1.1 Goals 35
4.1.2 Applications for SAN 36
4.1.3 Design Processes 37
4.1.4 SAN Topology 38
4.2 STORAGE VIRTUALIZATION 40
4.2.1 Virtualization Basics 40
4.2.2 Virtualization Levels 42
4.2.3 Virtualization Models 43
4.3 SECURITY 45
4.3.1 Zoning 45
4.3.2 Security Requirements 46
4.3.3 Access Control 46
4.3.4 Data Security 49
4.3.5 Encryption 50
4.4 ENCRYPTION METHODS 52
4.4.1 Data Encryption Standard 52
4.4.2 Advanced Encryption Standard 54
4.4.3 Diffie-Hellmann Algorithm 56
4.5 ENCRYPTION SYSTEMS 57
4.5.1 Public Key Infrastructures (PKI) 57
4.5.2 Other Certificate Options 59
4.5.3 Transport Layer Security (TLS) 60
4.5.4 Secure Shell (SSH) 61
4.5.5 Pretty Good Privacy (PGP) 61
4.6 OPERATIONAL CONSIDERATIONS 62
4.6.1 Cascading 63
4.6.2 Fabric Shortest Path First 64
4.6.3 Blocking 64
4.7 Latency 65
4.7.1 Oversubscription 65
4.7.2 Trunking 66
4.8 COST CONCERNS 66
4.8.1 Cost Contributors 67
4.8.2 Integrating Storage 67
4.9 REDUNDANT ARRAY OF INEXPENSIVE DISKS 68

4.10 BACKUPS ... 70
4.10.1 Full and Incremental Backups ... 71
4.10.2 Distributed and Centralized Backups ... 72
4.10.3 Data Replication ... 73
4.11 SAN MANAGEMENT ... 74
4.11.1 Strategies ... 75
4.11.2 Management Layers ... 76
4.12 CISCO FABRIC MANAGER ... 77
5 FIBRE CHANNEL ... 81
5.1 FIBRE LAYERS ... 81
5.1.1 FC-0 ... 82
5.1.2 FC-1 ... 82
5.1.3 FC-2 ... 83
5.1.4 FC-3 ... 86
5.1.5 FC-4 ... 86
5.2 FIBRE CHANNEL CLASSES ... 87
5.2.1 Class 1 ... 87
5.2.2 Class 2 ... 88
5.2.3 Class 3 ... 88
5.2.4 Class 4 ... 89
5.2.5 Class 5 ... 89
5.2.6 Class 6 ... 90
5.2.7 Class F ... 90
5.3 VSAN ... 90
5.3.1 Benefits of VSANs ... 91
5.4 FIBRE CHANNEL SECURITY ... 93
5.4.1 Fabric Security ... 93
6 CONFIGURATIONS ... 96
6.1 PRODUCT BASICS ... 96
6.1.1 Hardware Features ... 96
6.1.2 Software Features ... 97
6.1.3 Switch Management Features ... 97
6.1.4 Configuration Tools ... 98
6.2 COMMAND LINE INTERFACE ... 99
6.2.1 Command Modes ... 99

6.2.2 *Command Hierarchy* *100*
6.3 SWITCH CONFIGURATION 102
6.3.1 *Configuring the Switch* *103*
6.3.2 *Management Interface Configuration* *104*
6.3.3 *Software Upgrades* *105*
6.3.4 *Hardware Management* *106*
6.4 FIBRE CHANNEL INTERFACES 106
6.4.1 *Interface States* *106*
6.4.2 *Interface Configuration* *108*
6.4.3 *Graceful Shutdown* *109*
6.4.4 *SFP Transmitters* *110*
6.4.5 *Management Interface* *111*
6.5 CONFIGURING ZONES 112
6.5.1 *Implementation* *113*
6.5.2 *Configuration* *113*
6.5.3 *Creating Zone Sets* *114*
6.5.4 *Zone Enforcement* *115*
6.5.5 *Link Isolation* *115*
6.5.6 *Zone Database* *115*
6.6 SWITCH SECURITY 116
6.6.1 *Switch Management Security* *117*
6.6.2 *RADIUS* *117*
6.6.3 *AAA Services* *118*
6.6.4 *Role-Based Authorization* *119*
6.6.5 *Accounting Services* *120*
6.6.6 *SSH Services* *120*
6.6.7 *Administrator Password* *121*
6.6.8 *Cisco Access Control Server Configuration* *121*
6.7 SNMP CONFIGURATION 122
6.7.1 *Communities* *122*
6.7.2 *Contact Information* *122*
6.7.3 *Notifications* *122*
6.7.4 *SNMP Security Information* *123*
6.8 FIBRE CHANNEL ROUTING 124
6.8.1 *FSPF Solutions* *124*
6.8.2 *FSPF Information* *125*
6.9 IP SERVICES 126

6.9.1 Traffic Management 126
6.9.2 Access Control Lists 126
6.9.3 ACL Interface Application 130
6.10 DOMAIN PARAMETERS 130
6.10.1 Domain Phases 130
6.10.2 Domain Restart 131
6.10.3 Domain Configuration 131
6.11 SYSTEM MESSAGE LOGGING 132
6.11.1 Logging Facilities 132
6.11.2 Severity Levels 134
6.11.3 Logging Information 134
6.11.4 System Processes 135
6.11.5 System Status 135
6.12 COMMANDS 136
7 PRACTICE EXAM 150
7.1 REFRESHER QUESTIONS" 150
8 ANSWER GUIDE 165
8.1 ANSWERS TO QUESTIONS 165
9 REFERENCES 173
10 INDEX 175

1 *Cisco Certified Internetwork Expert*

Cisco Certified Internetwork Expert (CCIE) is the highest level certification for technical networking offered by Cisco. The CCIE certification can be taken in any of six career tracks:

- Routing and Switching
- Security
- Service Provider
- Storage Networking
- Voice
- Wireless

The track consists of a written exam and lab exams.

The Storage Network track of the CCIE certification includes the following topics:

- SAN Protocols
- SAN Requirements
- Fibre Channel Features
- IP Configurations
- IP Storage solutions
- SAN Management
- Cisco Storage Services
- Troubleshooting

2 Exam Specifics

Exams are delivered in a secure environment, proctored, and timed. Before taking any exam, individuals must accept the Cisco Career Certifications and Confidentiality Agreement online at the authorized testing center.

Exam questions require individuals to engage in problem solving tasks typically of networking operations. The types of questions possible on the exam include:

- Multiple choice single answer
- Multiple choice multiple answer

All exams are delivered through Pearson VUE. Questions are delivered in sequence and individuals cannot skip questions and return to them later. The test is 120 minutes and there are 90-110 questions.

A score report with a breakdown by exam section and score will be provided at the completion of computer-based exams.

Exams are scheduled up to six weeks in advance in the US and Canada. To schedule an exam, contact an authorized test delivery partner in the area. See www.cisco.com for registration information.

If an individual fails an exam, they must wait five calendar days before retesting.

2.1 Exam Prerequisites

CCIE candidates must have a CCNA (Cisco Certified Networking Associate) and BCMSN level knowledge to prepare for the CCDA exam.

3 *Storage Network Standards*

3.1 Fibre Channel Standards

3.1.1 Fibre Channel

Fibre Channel is a standard from the T11 Technical Committee of the InterNational Committee for Information Technology Standards (INCITS). The committee is accredited by the American National Standards Institute (ANSI). The technology has become the standard connection type for storage area networks (SEN) in enterprises because of its gigabits-speed networking capabilities.

Fibre Channel Protocol (FCP) is a transport protocol used to transport SCSI commands over Fibre Channel networks.

3.1.2 Topologies

Three major Fibre Channel topologies exist, which describe how ports within the network are connected. A port in Fibre Channel is any entity that actively communicates over the network. The topologies are:

- Point-to-Point – the simplest topology with limited connectivity, this topology describes two devices connected together.

- Arbitrated Loop – all devices are connected in a loop, any change to the loop because a device is added or removed from the loop results in all activity on the loop being disrupted. This includes any failure on the part of any single device. Hubs may exist to connect multiple devices together and bypass any failed ports.
- Switched Fabric – all devices or device loops are connected to Fibre Channel switches.

3.1.3 Fibre Channel Layers

Fibre Channel is a layered protocol similar to the OSI model for networks. It consists of 5 layers:

- FC0 – the physical layer
- FC1 – the data link layer
- FC2 – the network layer
- FC3 – the common services layer
- FC4 – the Protocol Mapping Layer

3.1.4 Fibre Channel Ports

The ports defined by Fibre Channel fall into several types, the first set are node ports while the general terms to summarize classes of ports:

- Node port (N_port)– a port on the node used in point-to-point and switched fabric topologies.
- Node loop port (NL_port) – a port on the node used in

arbitrated loop topologies.

- Fabric port (F_port) – a port on the switch that is connected point-to-point to a node.
- Fabric loop port (FL_port) – a port on the switch that is connected to an arbitrated loop.
- Expansion port (E_port) – a connection between two fibre channel switches to form an inter-switch link (ISL).
- EX_port – a connection between a fibre channel router and a fibre channel switch.
- Trunking e_port (TE_port) – a Cisco-based standard for an extended ISL (EISL) to allow for routing of multiple Virtual SANs.
- Auto port or auto-sensing port – can automatically switch between E_, TE_, F_, or FL_ port when required and found in Cisco switches.
- Fx_port – a generic port that can become a F_port or FL_port. Only found on Cisco devices where oversubscription is present.
- Generic port (g_port) – a switch operating as an E_port or F_port.
- L_port – any arbitrated loop port, NL_ or FL_.
- Universal port (U_port) – a term used for any arbitrary port.

3.2 SCSI Protocols

Small Computer System Interface (SCSI) is a set of standards for describing how to connect physical computing devices and transferring data between them. The standards define the commands, protocols, and interfaces.

3.2.1 SCSI Command

Within SCSI, communication exists between an initiator and a target. The initiator will send a command to the target. The command is sent in a Command Descriptor Block (CDB): a one byte operation code followed by five of more bytes defining the parameters of the command. The target then responds to the command with either success, check condition (error) or busy.

SCSI commands fall into four categories:

- N (non-data)
- W (writing data)
- R (reading data)
- B (bidirectional)

3.2.2 Logical Unit Number

At least one Logical Unit Number (LUN) is assigned to every device on the SCSI bus. A logical unit performs storage operations such as read or write. Each SCSI target provides one of more logical units that typically correspond to a storage volume. Though the LUN is strictly an identifier, it is often used to represent the logical unit.

The LUN is 64 bits in length and divided into four parts to reflect a multilevel addressing scheme:

- Controller ID
- Target ID
- Disk ID
- Slice ID

3.2.3 SCSI Protocol Layers

Data is transferred between devices on a SCSI bus through a protocol method. The process starts and ends on the same layer, similar to the process used in the OSI networking model. The layers are executed before data is transferred to or from another device. The protocol layers are executed again in the opposite direction after the data is transferred.

The protocol layers are often referred to as SCSI bus phases. The SCSI bus can only be in one phase at any given time.

The different phases are:

- BUS FREE
- ARBITRATION
- SELECTION
- MESSAGE OUT
- COMMAND OUT
- DATA OUT/IN
- STATUS IN
- MESSAGE IN
- RESELECTION

3.3 iSCSI

Internet SCSI, or iSCSI, is storage networking standard linking data storage devices using Internet Protocol. The standard allows SCSI commands to be carried over IP networks. Its greatest advantage is the ability to utilize existing IP-based network infrastructures. iSCSI uses TCP/IP to allow two hosts to negotiate and exchange SCSI commands.

3.3.1 SCSI Concepts

The initiator is an iSCSI client and can be hardware or software based. A hardware initiator is dedicated hardware with firmware to implement iSCSI. A software initiator uses code to implement iSCSI, usually within a kernel-resident device driver with a network interface card and network stack.

Both iSCSI initiators and targets have special names found within three name-formats:

- iSCSI Qualified Name (IQN) – iqn.yyyy-mmm
- Extended Unique Identifier – eui.(EUI-64 bit address)
- T11 Network Address Authority (NAA) – naa.(NAA 64-bit or 128-bit identifier)

An iSCSI device can be defined by several fields:

- Hostname or IP Address
- Port Number
- iSCSI Name
- Optional CHAP Secret

3.3.2 Internet Storage Name Service

Storage resources are located by iSCSI initiators using the Internet Storage Name Service (iSNS) protocol. iSNS allows for automatic discovery, management, and configuration of iSCSI and Fibre Channel devices on a TCP/IP network. The management services available to iSNS are similar to those found on Fibre Channel SANs.

The iSNS standard defines four components:

- Protocol – defines how clients and servers communicate.
- Clients – iSNS aware storage devices which initiate

transactions with iSNS servers. The iSNS clients register device attribute information in a common Discovery Domain (DD), gathers information from other registered clients and receive asynchronous notification of events occurring in the DD.

- Servers – initiate iSNS State Change Notifications and will store properly authenticated information in an iSNS database. They respond to queries and requests made by iSNS clients.
- Database – information repositories for iSNS servers storing information on client attributes.

The services provided by iSNS are:

- Name Registration and Storage Resource Discovery – all devices (initiators and devices) within a storage network can register and query an iSNS database.
- Discovery Domains and Login Control – used to divide storage nodes into management groups to limit the login process to a subset of appropriate targets registered in the iSNS. This limitation provides scalability by reducing the number of unnecessary logins and the time required to establish relationships between hosts and storage devices.
- State Change Notification – allows notifications to be issued from the iSNS Server about each event affecting storage nodes on the managed network.
- Bidirectional Mappings Between Devices – stores naming and discovery information about devices.

3.4 Internet Protocol

The Internet Protocol is a connection-less protocol used on packet-switched Link Layer networks. The protocol does not guarantee delivery, proper sequencing, nor avoid duplication, but relies on upper layer transport protocols, such as TCP to handle. IP, however, does provide header integrity achieved with a checksum.

Internet Protocol defines the addressing methods and structures for datagram (packet) encapsulation, which in turn can be used to ensure delivery of packets from a source host to a destination host based on addressing.

3.4.1 IPv4 Addressing

IPv4 uses 32-bit addresses written normally in dot-decimal notation consisting of four octets separated by a period. Over a billion unique addresses are possible through this schema. An IP address is divided into a Network ID and Host ID. All hosts on the same network have the same network ID. Each host has a unique host ID. The combination allows for unique identifiers (IP addresses) on a particular network. Computers, routers, and switches with multiple interfaces to the network have multiple IP addresses.

Classes of networks have been defined to allow a greater number of networks to be available. The specific classes are defined by:

- Class A – range of 1.0.0.0 to 126.0.0.0, where the first

octet is the network number and the remaining octets are the host address.

- Class B – range from 128.0.0.0 to 191.255.0.0, where the first two octets represent the network number and the remaining octets are the host number.
- Class C – range from 192.0.1.0 to 223.255.255.0, where the first three octets are the network number and the last octet is the host number.
- Class D – are reserved as multicast addresses and range from 224.0.0.1 to 239.255.255.255.
- Class E – are reserved for experimental networks and range from 240.0.0.0 to 254.0.0.0.

Though the IP address is typically represented using dotted decimal notation, it can also be represented in binary and Classless Interdomain Routing (CIDR) notations.

Binary formatting utilizes a 2-based numeral system, or bits within groupings of 8. Reading right to left each bit is twice the value of the preceding bit.

Examples

0000 0000 = 0

1111 1111 = 255

1111 0000 = 240

0000 1111 = 15

1010 1010 = 170

0101 0101 = 85

Binary translation

Code	1	1	1	1	1	1	1	1
Value	128	64	32	16	8	4	2	1

In dotted decimal format, xxx.xxx.xxx.xxx, the IP address can be represented in decimal (base 10) and hexadecimal (base 16) format. The addresses correlate to the binary address as such:

255.255.255.255 = 1111 1111.1111 1111.1111 1111.1111 1111
255.126.170.192 = 1111 1111.0111 1110.1010 1010.1100 0000

3.4.2 IPv6

IPv6 provides support to the unexpected growth of the Internet through a 128-bit address divided along 16-bit boundaries. Each 16-bit segment converts to a 4-digit hexadecimal number with a colon separating each number. The form of the address is xxxx:xxxx:xxxx:xxxx:xxxx:xxxx:xxxx:xxxx.

Zero-suppression makes address reading easier by removing any leading zeros from the address.

A subnet mask is not required with IPv6 because it uses a fixed prefix that contains specific routing and subnet information.

The benefits of IPv6 over IPv4 are:

- Large address space – provides every device on the Internet with a globally unique address.
- Efficient routing – supports hierarchical routing infrastructures.
- Straightforward configuration – uses Dynamic Host Configuration Protocol for IPv6 (DHCPv6) and local routers for automatic IP configuration.
- Enhanced security – provides better protection against address and port scanning attacks.

The subnet size for IPv6 is standardized to have a fixed host ID portion of 64 bits which will facilitate automatic formation of the host ID from the Link Layer MAC address.

IPv6 addresses are classified into three types:

- Unicast addresses – identifies a single network interface.
- Anycast addresses – assigned to a group of interfaces belonging to different nodes on the network. Delivery of a packet goes to the closest member interface.
- Multicast addresses – assigned to a group of interfaces belonging to different nodes on the network. Delivery of a packet goes to all the interfaces identified in the address.

To support translations and allow for networks to have both IPv4 and IPv6 addressing, the addressing format can be merged. Since the IPv4 address uses 32 bits, it uses the last two 16 bit segments of the

IPv6 address. The formatted address would look like:

xxxx:xxxx:xxxx:xxxx:xxxx:xxxx:yyy.yyy.yyy.yyy

Some IPv6 stacks will not support this mapped address feature.

3.4.3 Subnetting

Subnetting is a method used to determine the network, subnetwork, and hosts of an IP address. The default mask can be manipulated to create subnetworks for the LAN and WAN segments. Each call has a default address mask, which is a 32-bit string. The Network-layer devices use the IP address and the mask to determine which network portion the address belongs.

The strict rules of IP addressing cause a problem resulting in unused addresses. The description of the problem is shown through the following scenarios:

- A class C address range allows 254 hosts: a company of 40 hosts, 214 addresses would be wasted in the subnet.
- A class B address range allows 65,534 hosts: a company of 4000 hosts, 61,534 addresses would be wasted in the subnet.
- A class A address range allows 16,777,214 hosts: a company of 400,000 hosts, 16,377,214 addresses would be wasted in the subnet.

Class-less based IP addressing allows the default subnet mask to be extended which will change the representation of the host and network IDs. In a class B situation, extending the subnet mask by 2 bits, the host ID as 10 bits, while the network ID has 22 bits: the subnet is 255.255.192.0

To calculate the number of host IDs supported by the new subnet, use the formula '2^n-2' where n is the number of bits used for the host ID, so in the example above (2^{10}-2). To calculate the number of network IDs supported by the new subnet, use the formula '2^n-2' where n is the number of bits used for the network ID, so in the example above (2^{22}-2).

Using subnet masking, a large Class B network can be divided into smaller subnetworks. A /23 mask will create eight subnetworks; each network handling 510 hosts. One of these subnetworks can be divided even further with a /30 mask to provide 128 subnetworks to allow for serial links.

By converting the IP address and Mask into their binary notation and performing an XOR function, the subnetwork can be discovered. A Boolean AND results in a 1 if both bits are 1 and 0 in all other cases. For example - an IP address of 201.64.173.51 with a mask of 255.255.192.0 would be used to calculate as such:

201.64.173.51 = 1100 1001.0100 0000.1010 1101.0011 0011
255.255.192.0 = 1111 1111.1111 1111.1100 0000.0000 0000
= 1100 1001.0100 0000.1000 0000.0000 0000

The subnetwork result is 201.64.128.0.

A shortcut method for identifying the subnet will look for the interesting octet, the first octet of any importance. The mask octets of value 255 should copy the same octets for the IP address and the mask octets of the value 0 should copy 0 for the subnet address. Any remaining mask octet that is not 255 or 0 is the interesting octet. Subtract this value from 256 to find the key number, sometimes called the magic number. Find the integer multiple of the key number closet to, by not larger than the interesting octet's value. For example - an IP address of 198.54.169.55 with a mask of 255.255.251.0 would be used to calculate as such:

> 198.54.169.55 and 255.255.251.0 = 198.54.x.0
> x = the multiple 256-251 or 4 closest by not exceeding 169
> x = 168

The subnetwork result is 198.54.168.0.
To calculate all the subnets of a network, the binary approach and a simple decimal approach. In the binary approach, multiply the number of subnet bits by 2^n. Write down values for each binary value of 1 greater than the next until the number of subnet are reached and translate.

The decimal approach simply calculates similar to the key number. The difference between the number and 256 is than added to 0 until 256 is reached. For example - a network address of 201.64.0.0 with a mask of 255.255.192.0, would have the following subnets:

256-192 = 64

201.64.0.0

201.64.64.0

201.64.128.0

201.64.192.0

201.64.256.0 (invalid and discarded)

3.4.4 Classless Interdomain Routing

Though IP addresses are reallocated, routing tables have a problem reading the new subnet mask. To resolve the problem, a new format is required; hence the Classless Interdomain Routing (CIDR) Notation. CIDR Notation uses the Dotted Decimal Format and the number of bits used for the network ID.

255.255.192.1 would be written 255.255.192.1/22 or
1111 1111.1111 1111.1111 1100.0000 0000

192.23.4.15/18 would have a subnet notation dotted decimal as
1111 1111.1111 1111.1100 0000.0000 0000

In some cases, the number of available IP addresses on a network exceeds the number of computers. This is especially true for point-to-point serial connections. The additional unused IP addresses would be wasted. Variable Length Subnet Masks (VLSM) allows different masks to be used for different segments in the network.

CIDR is used within the Internet; within an organization, Variable-Length Subnet Mask (VLSM) is used. VLSM is used to manage the number of hosts available in a subnetwork. VLSM requires routing protocol supports sending of the subnet mask.

3.4.5 Supernetting

Where subnetting is used to divide IP address groups into smaller, more manageable groups, supernetting is a method for grouping networks into larger supernets through borrowing bits from the network portion of the address. This is especially important when the number of computers on a network exceed the number of addresses available, for example Class C networks with available 254 addresses.

By grouping two Class C networks together using supernets, more IP addresses are available. When two classful networks are grouped into a supernet, routing is now considered classless.

Address aggregation is a method of summarizing routing entries of a set of classful networks.

Classless Interdomain Routing (CIDR) is a function of Internet Border Gateway Protocol (BGP) routing to reduce the number of Class C routes from an autonomous system. This prevents several broadcasts messages each going to a single Class C networks from being sent out to the next router. Instead, a single broadcast message is sent to the autonomous system where it sends the message to the different networks.

3.4.6 Public and Private Addresses

Some addresses within the classes have been reserved for private use by companies in their internal network. These addresses cannot be routed to the Internet and are filtered out by Internet service provider. The private addresses in each of the classes are:

- Class A – 10.0.0.0 to 10.255.255.255
- Class B – 172.16.0.0 to 172.31.255.255
- Class C – 192.168.0.0 to 192.168.255.255

To connect to the Internet, a computer needs a globally unique IP address which is registered. For organizations, the IP address is used for Internet access and access to the organization's network. RFC 1918 provides a set of unregistered network numbers that are not used in the public domain, but can be used by organization for internal use.

3.4.7 Network Access Translation

RFC 1631 defines Network Access Translation, which allows organizations to use private IP address on an internal network and the Internet at the same time. This is done by using a valid registered IP address to represent the private address on the Internet.

Several variations of NAT are supported:

- Static NAT
- Dynamic NAT
- Overloading NAT with Port Address Translation (PAT)

With Static NAT, the IP addresses are statically mapped to each other, creating a one-to-one relationship between the registered address and the private address.

With Dynamic NAT, the one-to-one relationship between the registered address and the private address still exists. The registered addresses, or global addresses, are part of a pool of IP addresses which are dynamically used. Dynamic NAT defines criteria for determining how private addresses, or local addresses, should be translated.

With Dynamic NAT, an organization can have more local addresses than global addresses. When a packet arrives that needs a NAT entry, a global address is retrieved from the pool and associated to the local address. If no global address is available, the packet is discarded.

3.4.8 Port Address Translation (PAT)

Overloading allows NAT to support clients with a few global addresses. Port Address Translation (PAT) will translate the port number in addition to the IP address. With dynamic mapping, NAT provides a global IP address, but also a unique port number associated with that address. The NAT router keeps a table entry for every unique combination of local addresses and ports. With a 16-bit field for port numbers, overloading NAT provides more than 65,000 port numbers.

Though an organization has access to private addresses registered to them, they can also utilize network numbers registered to another organization. NAT will translate the source and destination IP addresses of two organizations using a network number if they are connected to the Internet. As the packet passes through the NAT router, the source and destination addresses are changed.

3.5 Fibre Channel and IP

3.5.1 Fibre Channel over IP

Fibre Channel over IP (FCIP) is a technology for storage networking developed by the Internet Engineering Task Force (IETF). The mechanisms of the technology enable Fibre Channel information to be transmitted through tunnels over IP networks. This is especially advantageous for data sharing in enterprises that are geographically dispersed and already have an IP network in place.

FCIP encapsulates the FC block data and transports it over a TCP tunnel. The services of TCP/IP establish the connectivity between remote Storage Area Networks, as well as any control and management of congestion. FC fabric services are not affected, nor are they replaced by IP.

3.5.2 Internet Fibre Channel Protocol

The Internet Fibre Channel Protocol (iFCP) transmits data to and from FC storage devices in a SAN or Internet using TCP/IP. The mechanism allows existing SCSI and Fibre Channel networks to be incorporated into the Internet. iFCP can be used in conjunction with FCIP and other FC protocols, or be a replacement of those protocols.

IFCP is a routed solution, where FCIP is a tunnel solution. The lower-layer FC transport is replaced with TCP.IP and Gigabit Ethernet. FC devices connect to an iFCP gateway or switch. The Fibre Channel session will terminate at the gateway and converts to a TCP/IP session through iFCP. The session reaches another gateway or switch and convert back to a Fibre Channel session. With this process, multiple FC SANs can be interconnected through an existing IP network.

IFCP is a gateway-to-gateway protocol. It uses TCP.IP switching and routing elements to complement the Fibre Channel SAN component. FC storage devices are assigned an IP address.

3.6 FICON

Fibre Connectivity, or FICON, is an IBM proprietary name for a FC layer 4 protocol used for mapping IBM's antecedent (ESCON) channel-to-control-unit cabling infrastructure and protocol onto standard FC services and infrastructure. The longer name for this protocol is the ANSI FC-SB-3 Single-Byte Command Code Sets-3 Mapping Protocol for FC.

Each FICON channel can support multiple concurrent data exchanges in full duplex mode. Information is transferred through FC sequences mapped as FICON Information unites (IUs). Each IU consists of one to four FC frames. The first frame carries 32 bytes of the FICON mapping protocol. There are four classes of IUs to conduct information transfers. The IU classes are:

- Command
- Transfer
- Data
- Response

4 Designing and Implementing SANs

4.1 Understanding the Customer

Storage Area Networks provide a solution for organizations to satisfy their storage needs. Because the options available to these solutions are numerous, choosing the right design can be a difficult effort. As the volumes of data increases in an organization, the features of a SAN can have a qualitative impact on the existing network. Storage Area Networks are not extensions of any enterprise network; rather they are a complete solution used in conjunction with the traditional network for purposes of storing data.

4.1.1 Goals

The needs of the organization are the first determinant for designing Storage Area Networks. An assessment of the existing network and requirements for future growth are important to discover. The implementation of a SAN requires investment and the proposed solution. An organization will generally have both business and technical goals that need to be considered.

Business goals typically focus on the benefits of a solution. For this reason, the existing storage solution should be analyzed to identify the problems that may be occurring. General problems may focus on lack of connectivity, problems sharing information, and lack of storage space, or constraints on bandwidth. These problems have an impact on the productivity and performance of the business.

In addition to the problems that an organization experiences, the costs and needs of storage may be making the existing management of the solution difficult. SAN solutions can assist in meeting business requirements ranging from on-demand storage to high availability solutions to supporting mission critical applications.

Availability, reliability, performance, manageability, and security are just a few factors that can measure and define the technical goals and requirements for the SAN solution. These factors work independently and cooperatively to impact the design of the SAN. Of all the factors, availability is typically the most prominent requirement because of the criticality of applications and hardware. When resources are unavailable to employees and customers alike, the loss of thousands, sometimes millions, of dollars could be at risk.

4.1.2 Applications for SAN

The general purpose of the SAN solution is to add bandwidth to specific applications and alleviate the burden of bandwidth on the primary network. As a technology, it can be applied to several networking applications including:

- Network Architecture
- Data Protection

- Data Interchange
- Clustering
- Data Valuing
- Disaster Recovery

One of the major implementations of SAN solutions is to externalize storage; that is to add a storage network to the existing network. This type of solution allows network-hosted applications to be easily executed. In addition, since much storage is required by multiple platforms, a single external solution can support several platforms without the restrictions of operating within the operating system.

4.1.3 Design Processes

Several design processes may be available for any given implementation; however, the general steps include:

- Assessment
- Planning
- Implementation
- Management

The first set is generally the assessment. The purpose of the assessment is to gather information about the current network and requirements. This starts with a site audit. The site audit will provide information about the technical, cultural, and business aspects of the design and implementation.

Part of the assessment is to take an inventory of the existing storage and server devices. How they are connected and configured is also important, since bad configurations may have additional concerns to overcome. Compatibility of hardware and software may restrict or enhance the options available.

4.1.4 SAN Topology

The general topology choices for SAN are:

- Point-to-Point
- Arbitrated Loop
- Switched Fabric

The simplest topology is the point-to-point connection, where a server is directly connected to a single disk array. The connection to the disk array can be implemented quickly and conveniently. However, it has several points of failure with the connection and therefore not considered reliable. Those ports of failure include the server, the disk array, and the cable.

Another hybrid version of the point-to-point connection is really an arbitrated loop. By adding another HBA to the server and connecting it to the disk array, a redundant connection is enabled. As a result, even if one of the HBAs, cables, or disk array controlled fail, the connection is still enabled. The only single point of failure is the server.

Adding another server with a single connection will increase the number of possible failure points. However, if the disk array support four controllers, redundant connections from the server will create two single points of failure. If either server fails, the entire chain fails. This topology now becomes an arbitrated loop.

To alleviate the problem of a failed chain, servers can be clustered. That is, the two servers can be linked together, resulting in one server being available even if the other fails. This configuration makes the clustered point-to-point connection the most reliable configuration for point-to-point connections.

In many enterprise setups, the SAN is an externalized network placed farther from the primary servers. In these cases, the concerns for distance and connections have to be considered. Adding an interconnect to the simple point-to-point connection; the topology becomes a Fibre Channel arbitrated loop. The interconnect serves as a hub between the servers and the disk array. Two connections are made from each server into the interconnect, with two connections from the interconnect to the disk array. The hub now becomes a single point of failure.

Add a second interconnect with connections to each server from each interconnect. This creates a system with no single point of failure. The system can be expanded by adding more servers, more hubs, and more disk arrays to meet the customer's needs. The hubs can be used to manage different areas of the storage array.

If distance is a consideration for connecting systems, the best interconnect device is a switch, making the management of the network easier. Latency is always a factor with distance, since it will increase directly proportional to the distance travels.

4.2 Storage Virtualization

Virtualization is simply an abstraction of computer resources. For many companies, virtualization raises the utilization of resources while reducing the cost of maintaining them. Consider several similar devices, such as storage, which are committed to specific application and are generally underutilized. Through virtualization, the storage space on each of the devices can be viewed as a single storage area and managed. As a result, physical storage space that is not used can be discarded.

4.2.1 Virtualization Basics

There are generally three activities that are virtualized: partitioning resources, combining resources, and emulation. One of the first forms of partitioning was on hard disks where a single physical device is broken down into several smaller volumes. Combining resources works in reverse, by combining several physical devices into one larger volume. Emulation is having one type of devices emulate, even enhance, the characteristics of another device: virtual memory is a form of emulation where physical memory acts as RAM.

In most solutions are combination of these activities are utilized. For instance, several physical hard drives are combines into a single logical hard drives, which is then logically partitioned into several smaller volumes. Many benefits are available through virtualization, including:

- Transferring functions rather than hot-swapping hardware in the event of failure.
- Running multiple copies of the same or different operating systems at the same time.
- Easier management and distribution of legacy applications.
- Ability to share a single server and its resources among multiple users as a “dedicated” resource.
- Failure in a virtualized instance does not impact other virtualized instances, as well as extremely quick recovery times.
- Ability to load balancing.
- Rapid development and testing of new software.

The use of virtualization techniques have been available since the 1960s and most commonly implemented by creating a 'virtual machine' to present an abstracted version of real computer hardware. For decades, virtualization has been primarily a software-based technology, but recently virtualization-friendly hardware features have been embedded into hardware designs, particularly server processors. The software provides a layer between the actual computing resources and the applications and network accessing those resources.

4.2.2 Virtualization Levels

Within a storage network, virtualization can be configured at different levels, namely:

- Fabric Level
- Storage Subsystem Level
- Server Level
- File System Level

At the fabric level, virtualization can allow the SAN to be zoned to allow the servers to see the virtualization appliances or the virtualization appliances to see the storage systems. As a result, the servers would not be able to see to operate the storage subsystems directly.

At the storage subsystem, disks can be divided into different LUNs using virtualization, essentially turning a single disk into multiple disks. The converse operation is also possible where multiple volumes are combined into one volume. RAID subsystems are an example of virtualization for storage.

Virtualization at the server level is possible through the logical volume management of the operating system. Individual servers do not control storage in a SAN and therefore any server can access the storage system. Capacity for a specific server can be added or removed when required without affecting the application servers. Storage management can be simplified and the cost of this management reduced.

The highest level of storage virtualization is at the file system level, because the data is shared, allocated, and protected appropriately, not just the volume that the data is on.

4.2.3 Virtualization Models

Storage virtualization is either in-band or out-of-band. Inside an in-band implementation, the data flow and control flow occur over the same path. The levels of abstraction exist in the data path. The domain manager controls a storage pool. No special software is required for the server.

Out of band virtualization has separate data flow and control paths. This is done by storing data in one place while storing information about the data, or meta-data, in another location. The meta-data includes all mapping and locking tables and it is moved to a separate server, usually called a meta-data controller. In this type of solution, the server will request authorization from the meta-data controller to the data it wants to access. Once that authorization is given, the server has access to the data without any additional intervention from the meta-data controller. The client who has made the original request to the server will then be able to directly input and output the data. The I/O can utilize the full bandwidth of the connection since all other requests through the meta-data controller is on another connection. This results in I/O performance nearly equal to the local file system performance.

The advantages of both in-band and out-band solutions are compared below.

IN-BAND	OUT-BAND
Provides SAN storage management	Provides SAN storage management
Performance optimizations performed in the data path	Relatively low overhead in data path
Able to off load functions from the host.	Able to off load functions from the host.
Integrates well with storage management software	Integrates well with storage management software
Supports multiple heterogeneous hosts	Supports multiple heterogeneous hosts
Releases customer from a particular vendor's storage	Releases customer from a particular vendor's storage
Integrates storage to create better management capabilities	Supports storage management from multiple vendors
Scalability excellent	Scalability excellent
Supports host systems not present in a cluster	

4.3 Security

4.3.1 Zoning

For any enterprise network, security is an immediate concern. For solutions such as SANS, the concern is compounded because of the need to ensure data stored is not corrupted intentionally or by accident, or be accessed by the wrong person. In many enterprises, certain groups have special or restricted access to the data available. In traditional storage solutions, restricted information was stored on file systems directly connected to a user's computer. With SAN solutions, the goal is to provide the privacy available with having local file systems while taking advantage of the cost and management reduction benefits of the centralized storage system.

A prominent solution to maintain privacy or data segregation within the SAN is to implement zoning. This technique enables the SAN to be segregations to support multiple operating systems, organizational groups, and individuals. The storage fabric enforces the separation of data as users attempt to communicate to the data which they have access. Zoning, itself, does not provide data security. However, it does provide the landscape for applying different levels of security to different sets of data.

4.3.2 Security Requirements

The concerns necessary to understand and define the security implementation within the SAN are:

- Prevention of control by hosts on all visible LUNs.
- Segregation of applications within the fabric.
- Segregation process and level of operating systems.
- Mechanism for allow access and denial of hosts to LUNs.
- Mechanism for switch-to-switch security.
- Prevention of unauthorized access.
- Mechanism for implementing different authorization levels.
- Mechanism for tracking, auditing, and making changes.

Security cannot interfere with the availability of the data.

4.3.3 Access Control

Typical access control architecture is comprised of three systems:

- Host
- Requester
- Authenticator

The services found within the architecture support the core attributes of the solution, including:

- Identification – provides identify
- Authentication – verifies identity and associated access

- Authorization – determines what actions are available to the user
- Accountability – tracks user activity

In security solutions, the host is a system, user, application, or service which provides the interface for identifying and authenticating the user. The requester, network access server (NAS), provides any challenges to the host used to verify the user. The authenticator provides the validation of the user's identity.

Identification ensures that the person requesting access is associated correctly with the role defined in the system. It is important for managing downstream activities and controls, such as accountability. The purpose of identification is to bind the individual user to the appropriate set of unique rights and privileges to required systems, applications, and services.

A person's identity is verified using authentication methods. When access a system, a person presents their unique user identification and additional data to establish trust between the user and the system. This combination can be as simple as a username and password. The system will authenticate the user and grant access if successful.

Common forms of identification include:

- Username
- User ID
- Account number

- Personal Identification Number (PIN)

Three essential practices for identification include:

- Uniqueness
- Nondescriptive
- Issuance

Identification for a user must be unique to the individual. A single person may possess several forms of identification, but each of them must be distinct from the others within a system. IDs should expose the role or job function of the user, especially those of:

- Admin
- Administrator
- Webmaster
- Finance
- Root

In situations where several access control environments exist that do not interact, share information, or provide access to the same resources; it is possible to duplicate the same user identification across those environments. Unfortunately, because individuals are prone to duplicating certain attributes such as passwords, it is typically bad security practice to allow a duplication of IDs.

The process used to issue identities must be secure and documented. The quality of the process will impact the quality of the identifier. An issuance process should consider:

- Approval

- Notification
- Administration
- Allocation

Authentication can utilize one, two, or all three factors, or types, to verify a user. There are three factors of authentication:

- By knowledge - what a person knows.
- By ownership – what a person has.
- By characteristic – what a person does or is.

4.3.4 Data Security

Security of the data focuses on two concepts: confidentiality and integrity. With confidentiality, the concern is to ensure that the information cannot be accessed by any person or system that is not authorized to access the information. Data encryption is often used to ensure that specific access is not available. Integrity of the data ensures that the data stored and/or processes is not altered or tampered with in any way.

Within a SAN implementation, the goal is to appropriately use the full functionality of the SAN without creating pockets, or islands, which partition the data.

4.3.5 Encryption

The two primary forms of cryptography to provide encryption are symmetric and asymmetric.

Symmetric ciphers utilize an algorithm that operates on a single cryptographic key that is used to encrypt and decrypt the message. This encryption process comes in many names:

- single key
- same key
- shared key
- secret key
- private key

The last two names represent the key factor in using symmetrical algorithms: securing the cryptographic key. The result is extensive focus on key management. This requires not only the generation of the key but also the secure transmission of the key to both the sender and receiver of the message. To ensure security, the key is often sent separate from the message itself, called out-of-band distribution.

Some of the more common symmetric algorithms are:

- Data Encryption Standard (DES)
- Advanced Encryption Standard (AES)
- International Data Encryption Algorithm (IDEA)
- CAST
- Secure and Fast Encryption Routine (SAFER)
- Blowfish

- Twofish
- RC5
- RC4

The idea behind asymmetric algorithms was introduced in 1976 by Drs. Whit Diffie and Martin Hellman. The idea utilizes two different keys link mathematically to perform cryptographic operations. Typically, one key is used to encrypt, while the other is used to decrypt.

These concepts were the introduction to public key cryptography. To use an asymmetric algorithm, a person would need to generate a key pair. One half of the key pair would remain secret known only to the key holder, called the private key. The other half of the key pair could be presented to anyone who wanted a copy, called the public key. Asymmetric algorithms are one-way functions.

Any message that is encrypted with a public key can only be decrypted with the private key of the pair, retaining the confidentiality of the encrypted message. This is because the sender would be encrypting the message with the public key of the receiver. Any message that is encrypted using the private key of the sender could be opened and read by anyone possessing the corresponding public key. The process allows the confidentiality of the message to remain intact and retain proof of origin. RSA is a form of asymmetric ciphers.

4.4 Encryption Methods

4.4.1 Data Encryption Standard

The Data Encryption Standard (DES) became a standard in 1977 when adopted by several US federal government agencies. Today, the encryption is used extensively in many financial, VPN, and online encryption systems.

The origins of DES are based on the work of Harst Feistal using the Lucifer algorithm. The core principle of the algorithm is to take an input block of plaintext and dividing it in half. Each half is then put through an XOR operation to alter the other half.

Each DES key is 64 bits in length with each eighth bit ignored, leaving an effective length of 56 bits.

There are five separate modes of DES, including:

- Electronic Codebook Mode (ECB)
- Cipher Block Chaining Mode (CBC)
- Cipher Feedback Mode (CFB)
- Output Feedback Mode (OFB)
- Counter Mode (CTR)

The DEC is a block mode cipher though the last three modes were developed to operate like a stream mode cipher in order to be more versatile and support stream-based applications.

ECB is the most basic mode of DEC. It encrypts each 64-bit block of text independently. It is used for very short messages.

With the CBC, the result of encrypting one block of data is used to encrypt the next block of data.

CFM will segment the input into blocks of 8 bits, or the size of one character. Each bit produced in the keystream is the result of a predetermined number of fixed ciphertext bits. The operation has the ciphertext result of the XOR calculations feed back in a shift register for the keystream.

In OFB mode, the keystream is generated independent of the message. The operation is the same as CFB, except that the encrypted keystream is feed into the shift register to create the next portion of the keystream.

High-speed applications use counter mode. It is named as such because a 64-bit random data block is used as the first initialization vector. This block is called counter and is different for every block of plaintext. Each subsequent counter is incremented by 1. The counter is encrypted and used as a keystream that is XORed with the plaintext. Since the keystream and the message are separate from each other; several blocks of data can be processed at the same time.

DES is susceptible to brute-force attacks because of the short key used. To overcome this weakness, a stronger version of DES was utilized by running the encryption process twice over the same plaintext message using different keys. This is commonly called as double DES.

Unfortunately, man-in-the-middle attacks are effective against double DES solution which led to the design of Triple DES. The solution utilizes two encryption keys and three encryption attempts. The plaintext message is encrypted using the first key, then the second, then the first key again.

Another mode of triple DES, EDE2, performs a decryption using the second key. Therefore the process used on the plaintext message is to encrypt using the first key, decrypt with the second key, then encrypt with the first key again. This mode is compliant to ISO 8732 and ANS X9.17.

EEE3 and EDE3 are triple DES modes utilizing three encryption keys.

4.4.2 Advanced Encryption Standard

In 1997, the National Institute of Standards and Technology (NIST) adopted the Advanced Encryption Standard (AES) as a replacement for DES and 3DES. The standard is based on the Rijndael algorithm created by Drs. Joan Daemon and Vincent Rijmen of Belgium. NIST chose AES after considering several possible candidates.

The Rijndael algorithm uses block sizes of 12 8, 192, and 256 bits with keys of the same lengths. The number of operating rounds used is related to the size of the key: 10, 12, and 14 respectively. AES supports only one block size.

To encrypt a plaintext message, the input is placed into a 128-bit state array while the key is placed into a similar table. Then, four major operations are conducted on the message:

- Substitute bytes – an S-box is used to substitute byte-by-byte on the entire block.
- Shift rows – each row in the table is offsetted.
- Mix columns – each value in a column is substituted based on the values of the data.
- Add round key – each byte is XORed with the key for the current round. Additional rounds are performed with a different key.

The most widely used form of public key encryption is RSA. Developed by Ron Rivest, Adi Shamir, and Len Adleman in 1978, RSA is based on factoring the product of two large prime numbers.

The formula used is:

$C = P^e \bmod n$ for encryption

$P = C^d \bmod n$ for encryption

To calculate RSA key pairs, two prime numbers are multiplied together:

n = pq

The public key is {e, n}. The integer e is relatively prime to (n) which is (p-1)(q-1)

The private key is {d,n}. The integer d is calculated using Euclid's algorithm: de = 10(n)+1

To attack the RSA algorithm, three major approaches are used:

- Trying all possible private keys.
- Factoring the product of two prime numbers.
- Measuring the running time if the decryption algorithm.

4.4.3 Diffie-Hellmann Algorithm

A key exchange algorithm used to enable two users to negotiate of exchange a secret symmetric key used for future encryption. It uses discrete logarithms based on finding the primitive root of a prime number.

Private and public keys are still used. The private key is randomly selected and must be less than the prime number. The two hosts would calculate the private key and a public key individually. The public keys would be exchanged and computer a common session key.

Once complete, the two parties could encrypt their data using a symmetric key.

4.5 Encryption Systems

4.5.1 Public Key Infrastructures (PKI)

The public key infrastructure (PKI) is a system of trust surrounding digital signatures: how they are created, distributed, and managed. It is used to establish trust between entities based on their mutual trusts of certificate authorities (CAs). SLL is not the only protocol or technology which builds on the PKI concept: X.509, IKE, and Virtual Private Networks (VPNs) also use PKI solutions.

The purpose of the PKI is to create a trusted relationship. This is possible only if the CA signing the peer's certificate is trusted. Trusting a CA involves obtaining and validating the CA's own certificate. After this validation, the details contained in the CA's certificate and its public key can be used to obtain and validate other certificates issued by the same CA.

A subordinate CA is a Certificate Authority that is certified by another Certificate Authority. Subordinate CAs can issue certificates to other subordinate CAs, creating a certification chain or hierarchy.

Enrollment is a process for requesting a CA to issue a certificate for an entity. The process begins with the generation of a key pair. A certificate request is created out of the public key and additional information about the module. The CA type will determine the type of certificate request created and the extent of the enrollment process.

When a certificate is received from another entity, the following process is followed to validate the certificate:

- Verify the certificate signature.
- Verify the certificate chain has not expired.
- Verify the certificate chain has not been revoked.

A computer will also validate the use of the certificate in a given situation, such as confirming the:

- Certificate is authorized to perform the required action.
- Correct certificate is used in the negotiation.

Two methods are used to determine the status of a certificate: CRL and Online Certificate Status Protocol (OCSP).

The CRL is available from either an HTTP server or an LDAP server. If the CRL repository is an HTTP server, the module uses the URL published in the CRL Distributed Point extension located on the certificate and opens an HTTP connection to access the repository. If the CRL is on an LDAP server, a computer will locate the CRL in one of the defined LDAP account units. If the CRL Distribution Point extension exists, the directory entry which the CRL is published or the LDAP URL is published. If the extension does not exist the attempt to locate the CRL is in the entry of the CA itself in the LDAP server.

OCSP allows applications to identify the state of a certificate and may be used to more timely information on revocations than possible using CRLs, as well as providing other status information. OCSP clients will issue a status request to the OCSP server, acceptance of the certificate is suspended until a response is received from the server. To use OCSP, the root CA must be configured to use this method instead of CRL and will be inherited by subordinate CA's.

4.5.2 Other Certificate Options

Using a PKI to generate and distribute a digital certificate is not the only option available. Other options include:

- Self-signed certificates
- Peer-to-peer certificates

In a self-signed certificate, a public/private key pair is used. The public key is placed into the certificate and the private key is used to sign the certificate. The certificate is associated with the application and distributed as users access the application. In this way, the organization deploying the application can become their own CA rather than depend on a public signing organization.

Peer-to-peer authentication is another method of establishing trust between two of more entities. It relies on one person who is trusted saying that another person they trust can be trusted. This extends until a network of trust is created.

4.5.3 Transport Layer Security (TLS)

Transport Layer Security is a cryptographic protocol which provides security for communications over the network by encrypting segments of the connection at the Transport layer. TLS is based on the Secure Sockets Layer (SSL) and is used in applications for web browsing, electronic mail, Internet faxing, instant messaging, and VoIP.

TLS is designed to prevent eavesdropping, tampering, and message forgery of Internet communications by providing endpoint authentication and communications confidentiality. TLS supports unilateral and bilateral authentication and involves three basic phases:

- Peer negotiation
- Key exchange and authentication
- Symmetric cipher encryption and message authentication

Different encryption algorithms can be used but must be agreed upon by both endpoints within a communication session.

TLS is used in conjunction with HTTP, FTP, and SMTP, tuning on top of them. It can be used with TCP or UDP. It is also used to create a Virtual Private Network by tunneling an entire network stack. SIP uses TLS to protect its application signaling.

4.5.4 Secure Shell (SSH)

A more secure protocol with the same functionality of Telnet, Secure Shell allows data to be exchanged using a secure channel between two networked devices. SSH is primarily used on Linux and UNIX systems to access shell accounts. Public-key cryptography is used to authenticate remote systems and the use, if needed. Often used to log into remote systems and execute commands, SSH will support tunneling, forwarding TCP ports and X11 connections.

SSH-2 has three well-separated layers:

- Transport layer – handles initial key exchange and server authentication and establishes encryption, compression, and integrity verification.
- User Authentication layer -handles client authentication and several methods for authentication including password, public-key, and keyboard-interactive.
- Connection layer – defines channels, channel requests, and global requests using SSH services.

4.5.5 Pretty Good Privacy (PGP)

The Pretty Good Privacy (PGP) protocol is used for privacy and digital signing of email messages, providing end-to-end security between sender and receiver. Traditionally, PGP performs key exchanges using RSA public key cryptography and encrypts messages using IDEA.

Within PGP, any user can validate the identity of another user, creating a network trust model. A user's public key can be obtained directly from the user then its hash can be communicated out of band. The keys are stored in files called key rings; public key rings can be found stored on the Internet.

4.6 Operational Considerations

Inter-switch links refers to the connection between the ports of one switch to the port of another switch. Frames originating from the node ports and from within the fabric is carried through the inter-switch links (ISLs). Frames generated from the fabric are used to control, manage, and support the fabric.

Before frames can be carried through the ISL, both switches have to complete a synchronization process where operating parameters are exchanged. If the operating parameter is not compatible, the switches cannot join and the ISL is considered segmented. In this state, the ISLs cannot carry any traffic originating on the node ports, but they cannot carry frames originating from the fabric.

Some of the other considerations in implementing ISLs are:

- Cascading
- Hops
- Fabric Shortest Path First
- Blocking

- Latency
- Oversubscription
- Congestion
- Trunking

4.6.1 Cascading

Cascading refers to the effort of expanding the fabric by interconnecting Fibre Channel switches and directors using ISLs. By cascading switches, the SAN environment can take advantage of the following benefits:

- Seamless extension of the fabric: switches can be added without having to power down the fabric.
- Distance between SAN participants can be increased.
- More switches can be added by providing more available ports.
- More resilience found in the fabric.
- Bandwidth can increase because frames between switches are delivered across all available data paths.
- Greater fault tolerance available within the fabric.

Traffic traveling from one switch to the next in an ISL is called a hop. Though cascading can expand the fabric, a hop count limit is set by the fabric operating system. The hop is used to derive a frame holding value for each switch, which is the maximum time allowed for a frame to be held in a switch before it can be dropped or the fabric is considered busy. The hop count limit should be investigated in any SAN design.

4.6.2 Fabric Shortest Path First

The fabric shortest path first (FSPF) is a link state path selection protocol which keeps track of the links on all switches in the fabric. Each link is associated with a cost and the paths from a switch to all other switches are computed by adding the cost of all links traversed by the path. The protocol then chooses the path is the least cost.

Hop count cost is what FSPF is based on. The link states and their cost for all switches in the fabric are compiled in a topology, or link state, database. The database is maintained on all the switches in the fabric and synchronized with all the switches. The initial database synchronization is performed when an individual switch is first initialized or when an ISL is established. When a link state change occurs, the update mechanism is used.

4.6.3 Blocking

Blocking occurs when data that is moved through the fabric by its components, switches or directors impacts the ports, targets, or initiators on the same fabric. Fabric components do not generally read the data they are transmitting. As a result, data is being received as it is being transmitted. During any single communication, up to 10 Gbps bandwidth can occur in each direction. To prevent any delay, non-blocking switch architecture is deployed on switches, directors, and hubs. Within this architecture, multiple connections are travelling concurrently through the internal components of the switch.

Blocking occurs when data does not get to its destination. If it does reach its destination, but is delayed, the effect is congestion. The non-blocking architecture is employed on switches and directors.

4.7 Latency

Latency is the time used by a frame to travel across the fabric. The more ISLs that are travelled, the more latency is acquired. In SANs, the traversal time does not normally include the time from between host and fabric or fabric and storage. The most common measurement is microseconds.

4.7.1 Oversubscription

Overscription is any situation where several ports are attempting to communicate with each other and the total throughput is more than a port can handle. The effect can occur on ISLs or storage ports. The possibility of oversubscription should be investigated when designing a SAN. Analysis of traffic patterns should uncover possible problem areas. Overcoming oversubscription on an ISL can be done by adding a parallel ISL. On a storage device, oversubscription can be dealt with by the addition of another adapter to the storage array.

4.7.2 Trunking

Switches have a feature called trunking which enables traffic to be distributed across the ILS while preserving in-order deliver. Some Fibre Channel protocol devices must have in-order exchanges of frames between the source device and the destination devices. As a result, a fixed route must be established. Certain traffic patterns can cause all active routes to be allocated to a single available path and leave other paths untouched.

Usually, a trunking group is created; that is, a set of available paths linking adjacent switches. The ports found within a trunking group are called trunking ports. If all the ISLs are gathered together as a trunk, they can be utilizes as a single, bigger ISL.

4.8 Cost Concerns

SANs allow for storage networks that are highly scalable and fast. Though the best technologies are always desired, cost effectiveness requires that business requirements be met and a reasonable return on investment obtained.

4.8.1 Cost Contributors

The cost of establishing and maintaining a SAN architecture are based on several contributing factors:

- Equipment – includes the interconnects, cables, and other devices required to upgrade or modify the existing configuration.
- Space – includes the physical floor space required for equipment, power, HVACs, and so on.
- Management – as another specialized network, SANs require additional resources to monitor and manage it. Training personnel in storage technologies is a major consideration for success.
- Establishment – the cost of implementation can sometimes be the greatest expense and dependent on political, cultural, and geographic considerations.

4.8.2 Integrating Storage

Storing data has two approaches:

- Distributed – utilizes multiple copies of the data and sometimes multiple locations. Data could be in several formats and available in multiple platforms. Distributed environments are beneficial to increase speed of access to a storage site. The costs of maintaining such environment is high because of the number of redundant storage devices and connections. The component of distributed environments that have the greatest costs are high-speed, high-bandwidth, and long-distance connections.

- Centralized – allows easier management and sharing of data while maintaining separate segments for different applications. All storage tasks are performed from a common management interface. High-speed access is available because resources are pooled into a single logical location, which also allows more efficient load balancing and sharing. Controlling storage virtualization is more effectively executed and changes performed with virtually no impact. Decision making-based on data usage is easily enabled.

4.9 Redundant Array of Inexpensive Disks

Each storage device involves different technologies. Tape devices are primarily used to back up large volumes of data. Magnetic disks are the preferred device for primary storage. Both technologies have the potential to fail at any point, though they are relatively stable. Redundant Array of Inexpensive Disks (RAID) provides a fault-tolerant array of drives to overcome any possibility of failure.

RAID is a simplified system for managing and maintaining the storage environment. The system creates a combined large storage device from smaller individual devices. Data is generally stored across different drives and different levels of RAID provide different levels of redundancy and performance. The most basic level is RAID 0. This level does not offer any redundancy and is not recommended for storing data. The different levels of RAID include:

- RAID Level 0 – simple level of disk striping which has data stored on all drives.
- RAID Level 1 – uses mirroring to replicate data from one drive to the next.
- RAID Level 3 – uses parity to store the parity value on a separate drive.
- RAID Level 5 – uses parity to store parity values across different drives.
- RAID Level 6 – parity is stored on striped drives along with the data.

The level of redundancy provided by a virtual disk ensures that the data is protected from disk failures. Damaged drives can be hot-swapped without disrupting the network functions. The technology is for large database operations, and RAID 5 and RAID 3 options are the most popular choices for large databases.

Software implementation of RAID is possible, but the write speeds are typically slower than hardware implementations. The reason for this reduction in speed is the need for the host system to calculate the parity values and perform additional I/O operations to ensure the storage of these values. To minimize host processing, fast RAID arrays have additional hardware caches, multiple buses, and striping schemes.

Back to the different RAID levels, deciding which level to use is one of the most important decisions in SAN designing using RAID. Level 0 is best used when high throughput is desired with the lowest cost possible, but offers no redundancy. Level 1 is excellent when the primary requirements are high availability and high reliability, but is costly since double the storage capacity is required. RAID level 3 provide the best high data transfer and costs less than other levels, but write performance is low and is unsuitable for frequent transactions using small data transfers. Level 5 has a high read rate and is reliable. It is most suitable for multiple applications, but performance goes down when the drive fails though it can withstand single drive failures. Level 6 have high reliability and high read speed. It is best used when the primary requirements are high availability and data security. The costs are high and the write speed is slower than RAID 5.

4.10 Backups

Backups are activities where data is copied to a second location for the purpose of archiving and recovery. Tape devices are the primary means for storing backup data because it is inexpensive and physically compact. Unfortunately, storing data on tape is susceptible to errors, the process of recording is slow and tapes can be damaged. Disk storage provides an alternative to tape drives.

As organizations grow, so does the data that needs to be backed up.

Traditionally, backups were often performed late at night when general office hours were over. Globalization and 24 hour operations have made backup scheduling even more difficult.

Backup architectures provided by SANs offer:

- Reliability through the tape mirroring.
- Availability and performance through clustered servers.
- Remote connections to perform backup activities.

4.10.1 Full and Incremental Backups

A full backup will back up all the data blocks in the datafiles, whether they are modified or not. An incremental backup will only back up the data blocks in the datafiles that were modified since the last incremental backup. A full backup cannot be part of an incremental backup strategy. The baseline backup for an incremental backup is designated as level 0. This level 0 backup is a full backup since all blocks are backed up regardless of modification. Incremental backups are then merged with the level 0 backup in the future to complete a full backup at the current point of time.

Two types of incremental backups exist:

- Differential
- Cumulative

A differential incremental backup will back up only data blocks modified since the more recent backup at the same level of lower. An occurrence of the level 1 or level 2 backup is determined and any modifications made since the last backup is included. This is the default method for incremental backups.

A cumulative incremental backup will back up the data blocks that have been modified since the most recent backup of the next lowest level, or n-1. As a result, only one cumulative incremental backup needs to be restored rather than multiple differential incremental backups. A cumulative incremental backup requires more space than a differential incremental backup.

4.10.2 Distributed and Centralized Backups

Conventional methods of backing up data fall into two types: distributed and centralized. Distributed methods attach backup devices to every server. In a centralized solution, the backup device is connected to a central machine and backups are performed over the LAN.

Distributed backups are the fastest method of backing up a server's internal disk drive. It is the most appropriate solution for small network environments. As the network grows and more servers are added, the distributed process becomes more complicated and uses more tape drives.

In a centralized solution, the IP network supports the communication between servers and the centralized backup repository. The downfall to this type of solution is the consumption of server CPU resources required to transfer the complete volume which is taken to the maximum extent. This sometimes refers to poor server performance.

Backup solutions which utilize a SAN take advantage of a dedicated storage network to enable the process. As a result, all the benefits for managing backups that are present for a centralized backup method still exist.

4.10.3 Data Replication

Data replication is another form of backing up data which copies data in different forms. Replication allows multiple copies of the same data to be stored and accessed in multiple locations throughout the enterprise. This increases the overall performance of the network in accessing the data, while ensuring that if a single location fails, the data is still accessible from another location.

Replication of data is a popular solution for disaster recovery and globalization requirements because of its support of high availability needs. Replication is either performed at the storage level or application level. Storage replication refers to bulk transfers of data belonging to one application on one server to another server or set of servers. Storage replication occurs irrespective of the application it replicates and allows multiple applications to run on a single server. Application replication focuses on the storage replication of a single application. The application performs the replication at the transactional level. When multiple applications exist on a single server, each application requires their own application-specific replication.

Replication can be synchronous or asynchronous. The synchronous mode has data written faster because the backup process takes over the host until it is complete. This of course presents performance delays in other operations for the host. With asynchronous replication, the signal for completion is not required and interruptions can occur without disrupting the backup. Some operations may switch between modes, starting in synchronous mode until a communication problem occurs where the operation switches to asynchronous mode.

4.11 SAN Management

SAN Management is a requirement for ensuring the implementation of common standards across multiple devices. The discipline is a combination of network management and storage management. The implementation of SAN management will differ as different components and technologies are included in the SAN.

SAN management is dependent on the decisions for organizing data. The structure of the data storage is guided by:

- Storage policy
- Application-based storage
- Criticality

Also guiding the implementation of data management and ultimately SAN management is the quality of data; that is, the accuracy of the data. When multiple users have access to the data, specifically to change it, the potential for the data to be accurate over time decreases. The management system must ensure data integrity is maintained.

4.11.1 Strategies

Strategies for SAN management focus on managing the network in-band or out-band. In-band management refers to the process of direction communicating management information between storage and the processor. Out-band management is the process of communicating the same information without relying on the topology.

The subsystems of a SAM include servers, infrastructure, and storage devices. The infrastructure consists of interconnects and provides some of the information required to manage the SAN. Information from the servers and the storage devices is also important to provide a complete picture for end-to-end management. However the ability to segregate the information between the subsystems allows management decisions to effective obtain the appropriate actions required. The three tasks of the management system involve:

- Failure notification
- Prediction
- Prevention

4.11.2 Management Layers

Storage management systems are classified into five layers:

- Application Management – focuses on the availability and performance of the application on the network; specifically preserving the application's ability to function even when a device fails. Applications can be monitored, controlled, and managed through a consolidated graphical interface.
- Data Management – focuses on preserving the quality of data as it is transmitted and stored on the network, including ensuring its availability and accessibility. At this layer, all movement and management of data begins, including backups. Policies determine automated tasks, distribution, and criticality levels of the data.
- Resource Management – focuses on the management of devices to ensure the optimal utilization of all resources. A panel display attached to each device will provide basic information on the device's status. A resource manager will provide a single console to monitor all devices from a central location. Resource management allows devices to be shared across several applications.
- Network Management – maps all the physical components of a SAN and enables in-band and out-band management to be performed. At this layer, zoning is performed. The primary focus of network management is the assurance that the network remains available at all times and is fully

optimized.

- Element Management – focuses on the specific disk subsystems, removable media, and interconnects existing in the network. Fabric management is a component of element management and utilizes either in-band or out-band management. In-band management at this layer focuses on the direct transmission of information between devices and the management facility. The transmission across the FC connection uses the SCSI Enclosure Services (SES) protocol. Crucial topology information is maintained on the switch to assist in routing information and requests. Out-band management uses SNMP as the protocol to communicate between devices and management facility without relying on the fabric.

4.12 Cisco Fabric Manager

The Cisco Fabric Manager is used to manage the Fibre Channel components of the storage network. The basic components of the Fabric Manager are:

- Fabric Manager Server
- Fabric Manager Client
- Device Manager
- Fabric Management Web Client
- Performance Management
- Traffic Analyzer

- Authentication
- Network Monitoring
- Performance Monitoring

The Fabric Manager Server provides centralized MDS monitoring, troubleshooting, and configuration capabilities. Fabric information is collected using SNMP. Each computer configured with the Fabric Manager can monitor multiple FC SAN fabrics, supporting up to 16 concurrent clients.

The Fabric Manager Client is Java and SNMP-based. This network fabric and device management tool provides troubleshooting capabilities the FC.

The Device Manager shows the detail values for a single switch, incorporating graphical representations of the chassis, switching modules, supervisor modules, port status, power supplies and fan assemblies. Two views are available: the Device View and the Summary View. Interfaces on the switch can be monitored in the Summary View. The Device View allows switch-level configurations for:

- Virtual FC interfaces
- FCoE features
- Zones for multiple VSANs
- Managing Ports, PortChannels, and Trunking
- Managing SNMPv3 security
- Managing CLI security

- Managing alarms, events, and notifications
- Configuration file management
- Displaying hardware configurations

The Fabric Manager Web Client allows switch events, performance, and inventory to be monitored from a remote location using a web browser. Available to the Web client are performance manager summary reports, performance manager drill-down reports, and a zero maintenance database.

Performance Manager will gather historical statistics for network devices and provide graphical representations of the statistics through a web browser. The tool operates in three stages: Definition, Collection, and Presentation. Statistics can be collected for ISLs, hosts, storage elements, and configured flows.

Real-time analysis of traffic can be provided by the Cisco Traffic Analyzer through a Web browser. The Traffic Analyzer will monitor:

- Response times
- SCSI I/Os per second
- SCSI read or traffic throughput
- Frame counts
- SCSI session status
- Management tasks

Authentication in Fabric Manager utilizes a user name and password. The credentials are placed in the Fabric Manager Client and passed onto the Fabric Manager Server to authenticate to the seed switch selected in the client. If the credentials are not recognized, a CLI session is opened to the switch and retried. If recognized, a temporary SNMP user name is created to be used in the Fabric Manager system.

Network Monitoring from the Fabric Manager provides extensive discovery, topology mapping, and information viewing. The information is collected through SNMP queries. From these queries, the fabric topology is recreated and displayed in a customized map as well as several viewing options. Performance monitoring is provides through multiple tools within the Fabric Manager and Device Manager.

5 *Fibre Channel*

Fibre Channel is a technology standard that allows data to be transferred at high speed as great as 10 GBps. The standard is accredited by ANSI. The technology consists of an interface that is three times faster than SCSI. Fibre Channel can work on any type of cable, not just fiber optic for which it was originally designed. Some refer to Fibre Channel as the Fibre version of SCSI. This architecture is used to carry IP, IPI, FICON, and FCP traffic on the standard FC transport.

5.1 Fibre Layers

The Fibre Channel has five layers, similar in concept to the OSI model. Each layer can be developed independently from the adjacent layer. The five layers are categorized in two parts: the physical layer and upper layers. From top to bottom, here are the layers:

- FC-4 – Protocol Mapping Layer (Upper Layer)
- FC-3 – Common Services (Upper Layer)
- FC-2 – Signaling Protocol (Physical Layer)
- FC-1 – Transmission Protocol (Physical Layer)
- FC-0 – Physical Interface /Media (Physical Layer)

5.1.1 FC-0

The lowest layer defines the physical components of the system from cabling to connectors to electrical parameters. The level is designed to provide flexibility. A number of technologies can be used to meet the organization's needs. These technologies are used to create links in a communication route from a source to a destination.

The layer also provides a safety system for laser data links, called the Open Fibre Control (OFC) system. The system was designed to prevent optical power levels exceed the limits defined by laser safety standards. If a fibre connection is broken, a series of pulses are sent by the ports until the physical break is repaired. With a restored connection, handshake procedures are performed to re-establish the connection. This process acts as safety lock for point-to-point fibre connections.

5.1.2 FC-1

The transmission protocol layer, FC-1, focuses on methods in adaptive 9B/10B encoding. At this layer, data and clock information is integrated for use with serial transmission technologies. The encoding performed enables binding of the maximum length of code, maintains DC-Balance, and provides work alignment. DC-Balance speaks to an adjustment for ensuring that any noise is removed which is present in the transmission because of additional voltage.

The transmission protocol transmits information 8 bits at a time in a 10-bit transmission character, using special serial encoding and decoding rules, characters, and error control. The code being generation must be compatible with the electrical requirements of the receiving units, so must be DC-Balanced. The encoded information byte is in hexadecimal format. Each transmission character is named in the Zxx-y format where Z is the control variable, xx is the decimal equivalent of the binary numbers E, D, C, B, and A and y is the decimal equivalent of binary numbers G and H.

5.1.3 FC-2

The third layer of Fibre Channel and top layer of the physical layer is FC-2. The layer specifies the mechanisms for data transport independent of the upper layer protocols. Several types of environments are supported including point-to-point, arbitrated loop, and switched environment. FC-2 is self-configuring.

The transport mechanisms defined determine:

- Communication models
- General fabric model
- Topology
- Service classes
- Sequence and exchange identifiers
- Segmentation and reassembly

The framing protocol determined the framing rules used to transmit data. The set of rules include:

- Ordered Set
- Frame
- Sequence
- Exchange
- Protocol

The transmitted data is done in 4-byte ordered sets which provide access to bit and word synchronization and establish a word boundary. The ordered sets contain data and control characters. Each ordered set begins with a special character and are divided into three types:

- Frame delimiters – precede or follow the frame and signify the beginning or end of the frame. It includes start (SOF) and end (EOF) ordered sets.
- Idle ordered sets- a signal sent to notify the availability of a port to accept frame transmissions.
- Receiver Ready ordered set 0 a signal sent to notify the availability of an interface buffer for receiving frames.

The basic components of a Fibre Channel connection is the frame, which contains the information to be transmitted, as well as additional information specifying where and how the information should be transmitted. Broad classifications of frames include Data frames and Link_control frames. Data frames are further classified into Link-Data and Device_Data frames. The frames are transported across the fabric which receives them from the source port and delivers to the destination port. Once delivered, the frames are reassembled.

The frame begins and ends with a Frame Delimiter. Following the initial delimiter, the optional frame header contains information for control and links. This information is 64-bytes. The payload per frame is fixed at a maximum of 2112 bytes and contains the actual information being transported. A 4-byte Cyclic Redundancy Check (CRC) error check comes before the final delimiter.

A set of frames transported unidirectionally from one port to the next make up a sequence. All frames within the set are numbered with a sequence count.

A single operation determines the exchange in terms of one or more non-concurrent sequences. An exchange can be unidirectional or bidirectional. Sequences make up the exchange, though only one sequence can be active at any given time. Additional exchanges running simultaneously can allow multiple sequences to be active.

Protocols refer to higher-layer services. Fiber Channel has its own set of protocols to manage data transfer. Also specified in the standard are the following protocols:

- Primitive Sequence Protocols – for link failure.
- N_Port Login Protocol – for exchanging service parameters between ports.
- Fabric Login Protocol – for interchanging service parameters between port and fabric.

- N_Port Logout Protocol – for requesting removal of the service parameter information from the other port.

5.1.4 FC-3

FC-3 defines the functions that are available on multiple ports on a single node or fabric. The currently supported functions include:

- Hunt groups – a set of associated N_ports attached to a node and assigned an alias identifier. Any frame containing the alias can be routed to any available N-port in the set.
- Striping – uses multiple N-ports in parallel to increase bandwidth for transmitting a single information unit across several links.
- Multicast – delivers a single transmission to multiple destination ports.

5.1.5 FC-4

FC-4 provides application-specific protocols. It allows the concurrent transport of network and channel information over the same physical interface. The mapping rules for Upper Layer protocols are specified in FC-4. Protocols mapped to the Fibre Channel transport service consist of IP, FCP, and FICON.

5.2 Fibre Channel Classes

The standard for Fibre Channel defines several service class options, which control the flow control and can be used to optimize the functioning of Fibre Channel systems. Each class represents a mode of operation appropriate for a set of applications. Six kinds of classes are defined. The most commonly used are the first three classes.

5.2.1 Class 1

A Class 1 refers to the establishment of a dedicated end-to-end connection through the fabric, creating the equivalent of a dedicated physical connection. After being established between two ports, Class 1 guarantees that the connection will provide the maximum bandwidth. The connection remains stable until it is completed. Any additional requests for a connection with the same port are automatically denied.

Another guarantee of Class 1 is the arrival of each frame to the destination port in the same order it was sent. The receiving port will acknowledge every frame. This type of connection is useful for applications that are bandwidth-sensitive and require the full use of available bandwidth. The disadvantage is that if the application does not use the available bandwidth, it simply sits idle and unusable by other applications. Class 1 connections are therefore considered blocking connections which can disrupt a busy fabric.

5.2.2 Class 2

Class 2 provides a frame-switched connectionless service. Bandwidth is shared. A robust link between ports similar to Class 1 is enabled, as well as the ability to multiplex framed from several devices to be shared over one or many channels. A switch connection is used to create simultaneous exchanges.

Frames within a Class 2 system can be routed through the fabric and each frame can take a different route. As such, delivery of the frame in a specific order is not guaranteed. The receipt of every frame is still acknowledged by the destination port. If a frame is not delivered, a busy frame is sent to the source device to initiate the resending of the message.

Class 2 systems are best for mass-storage applications, server clustering, and other applications for mission-critical operations. It is not appropriate for using SCSI protocols over Fibre Channel since SCSI requires that frames be delivered sequentially.

5.2.3 Class 3

Within Class 3 systems, the characteristics of class 2 exist except for the acknowledgment of received frames. It provides buffer-to-buffer flow control to prevent loss of frames in transit. Data transferred to the buffer of the destination device can sometimes be overwritten and therefore upper-layer protocols are required to perform error recovery processes or request resending of dropped frames.

Fibre Channel devices have the option in Class 3 to broadcast messages to all multicast group members, enabling a device to transmit simultaneously to multiple recipients.

5.2.4 Class 4

Class 4 is similar to Class 1 as a connection-oriented service. It is different in that only a part of the available bandwidth is allocated between two N-Ports. To guarantee Quality of Service (QoS), virtual circuits (VCs) can be established. In-order delivery of frames is guaranteed, as well as acknowledgment of delivered frames. Within a Class 4 system, the fabric is responsible for multiplexing frames from different VCs. These systems are appropriate for multimedia applications or applications that allocate an established bandwidth by department.

5.2.5 Class 5

Class 5 systems are for applications that require immediate delivery of the data as it arrives, and therefore, no buffering. It is called isochronous service. Its definition is not clear and is not included in FC_PH documents.

5.2.6 Class 6

Another variant of class 1 is a class 6 system, also known as a multicast class of service. Dedicated connections for a reliable multicast are provided. A class 6 connection may be request by an N-Port for one or more destinations. A multicast server from within the fabric will establish the connection and obtain any required acknowledgments from the various destinations. Once a connection is established, it is retained and guaranteed by the fabric until the communication ends. This type of system is appropriate for audio and video applications requiring functionality.

5.2.7 Class F

Class F is an additional class of service defined in the FC-SW and FC-SW-2 standard. If is used by switches communicating through ISLs. It is a connectionless service with notification of non-delivery. The system is similar to class 2 except that class F deals with E-ports for control and management of the fabric.

5.3 VSAN

Virtual SANs are a collection of ports associated with a set of connected Fibre Channel switches to form a virtual fabric. Multiple VSANs can be partitioned through different ports on a single switch. In the same conceptual manner of virtualization, multiple switches can join several ports together to form a single VSAN.

The design of VSANs originated with Cisco and modeled after the concept of virtual LANs. VSANs can offer different protocols and operate as a separate self-contained fabric using conventions such as security policies, events, zones, memberships, and name services. While a fabric will resize based on the switch, a VSAN is resized based on port.

Because VSANs are isolated from each other, problems that occur with one VSAN will not have any impact on other VSANs. Additionally, each VSAN can be configured different from one another.

5.3.1 Benefits of VSANs

The benefits available by using VLANs include:

- Virtual SAN Islands – VSANs provide a way to consolidate multiple costly physical SAN islands into a common redundant SAN fabric, allowing the same security and isolation to be achieved and replicated virtually within the same physical environment.
- Transparent to End Devices – As traffic enters a switch, it is tagged. The tag is removed when the frame leaves a switch. No special awareness, configuration, or software is required to support a VSAN.
- ISL trunking – Using TE_Ports, VSANs can be trunked. While traffic cannot travel across a VLAN, multiple VSANs

can share the same ISL. Trunking allows a basic form of traffic shaping to be implemented.

- Fabric Availability – Each VSAN is implemented with separate instances of all fabric services. As a result, the fabric is more stable. Even fabric level events are isolated for each VSAN. If a switch is added to the existing infrastructure, only the affect VLAN(s) will be affected. Disruptions are isolated to individual environments with a resultant increase in availability that can enable larger, more cost efficient SANs.
- Fabric Scalability – Several limitations are present to prevent Fibre Channel from being scaled. The implementation of VSANs can overcome these limitations by allowing a FC address scheme to be present for each VSAN. On its own, a standard fabric supports only 239 domains (switches). With VSANs, 239 domains can exist for each VSAN.
- Collapsed Physical Infrastructure – Each application, operating system, or business unit can have its own VSAN, enabling a decrease in hardware costs and an increase in the manageability of the network.

5.4 Fibre Channel Security

5.4.1 Fabric Security

Fabric security utilizes several methods that build on the traditional methods of securing a network. Of importance to fabric security is:

- Fibre Channel Authentication Protocol
- Virtual SANs
- Zoning
- LUN masking
- Persistent binding
- Port binding

Fibre Channel Authentication Protocol (FCAP) is an extension of Switch link Authentication Protocol (SLAP) to establish a region of trust over the entire SAN domain. The region of trust provided by SLAP focuses on the area between two switches and did not extend into the SAN. PKI-based cryptographic authentication is utilized by FCAP to establish a common region of trust among different entities such as HBAs and switches.

A central third party guarantees the trust built, using a certificate exchanges. A fabric authorization database exists with a list of World Wide Names (WWNs) and associated information to allow switch authorization to the fabric. An entry within the authentication database will contain at least the switch WWN, the authentication mechanism identifier, and the list of authentication parameters to control access.

Cisco's Virtual SAN (VSAN) technology became an industry standard by the American National Standards Institute in 2004. The technology enables a single physical fabric into several logical SANs working independently. The individual VSANs can overlap within the physical fabric infrastructure, but contains dedicated fabric services for scalability, resilience, and operational independence. Each VSANs has its own hardware-enforced zones and management capabilities, but allow more efficient SAN utilization and flexibility through allocation and sharing among uses and segregation of traffic and control of resource domains.

Zoning provides further segmentation of the switched fabric. It is most useful when creating barriers between different environments. Members of one zone can only communicate within that zone. Though zoning doesn't provide security, it does provide separate environments to manage disparate systems and applications with conflicting security techniques. It also provides flexible management of a switched fabric to meet different user group objectives.

Zoning is implemented by hardware or by software and can be used in conjunction with each other. Hardware zoning is based on a physical fabric port number, with members of the zone being physical ports on the fabric switch. The switch hardware used will determine the level and features of hardware enforced zoning. A single port can belong to multiple zones. Software zoning is possible through fabric operating systems within the switches. Members of the zone are defined by their WWN or WWPN. A device's physical connection to a switch has no impact to software zoning, allowing them to be a member of the zone even if the device is connected to a different physical port.

LUN masking is an effort to prevent hosts from taking over resources already assigned. Every storage device presents its resources to the hosts through the use of LUNs. If a host must access the storage, a request is made to access the LUN. LUN masking controls the access to these LUNs.

Persistence binding speaks server-level access control which uses configuration information to drive the operations of the server's HBA driver. The configuration binds a server device name to a specific Fibre Channel storage volume or LUN. For a higher level of security, use port binding to bind a device to a particular port.

6 Configurations

The following sections are based on the Cisco MDS 9020 Fabric Switch. Other Cisco products may have similar implementations of the same features. Check specific product guides for reference when configuring the system.

6.1 Product Basics

6.1.1 Hardware Features

The following hardware features are found on the Cisco MDS 9020 Fabric Switch:

- 20 4-Gbps Fibre Channel ports per 1 RU
- Autodiscovery of FC connections
- Autonegotiation of port Transmission speeds
- Port interfaces supporting small-form-factor pluggable (SPF) transceivers that can be replaced in the field and hot swapped.
- Front to back airflow
- Cisco MDS 9000 FabricWare software
- Full compatibility

6.1.2 Software Features

- Switch Reliability – ensures continued service with no degradation to provide power-on self testing (POST), detect errors, isolate faults, perform parity checking, and display LEDS for status on power.
- Intelligent Zoning – controls access between devices by partitioning devices using different operating systems, creating logical sets of closed user groups, and configuring groups of devices separately from the rest of the fabric.
- IP Services – supports IP over Ethernet for traffic management and Network Time Protocol (BTP) servers.

6.1.3 Switch Management Features

Additional management features fall into two categories:

- Fabric Management
- Security Management

Fabric Management is performed through the command-Line interface (CLI) using Telnet, SSH, or a serial console or through the Fabric Manager using the Simple Network Management Protocol (SNMP).

Secure switch management enables user authentication and roles. Each switch can be accessed using the CLI or Fabric Manager to provide:

- Secure switch access – controlled security through data encryption, user Ids, and passwords.
- IP access control lists (IP-ACLs) – restrict IP-related out-of-band management traffic based on IP addresses to control transmissions on management interfaces.

Authentication, authorization, and accounting (AAA) is the strategy used to verify the identity of remote users, grant access, and track activities. Authentication is based on roles to limit access to switch operations by assigning roles to users.

6.1.4 Configuration Tools

The Command Line Interface (CLI) allows commands to be entered at the switch prompt. The CLI parser provides command help, command completion, and keyboard sequences to access previously executed commands.

The Fabric Manager application is a set of tools for network management that supports SNMP. It provides a graphical user interface (GUI) to display a real-time representation of the network fabric. The network management tools include:

- Fabric Manager Server – enables advance monitoring, troubleshooting, and configuration for multiple fabrics to show all servers running when the application initiates.
- Device Manager – provides a device view of the switch to

display a continuous updated physical representation of the switch configuration and provide access to statistics and configuration information for a single switch.

- Fabric Manager Web Client – allows operators to monitor MDS events, performance, and inventory from a remote location.

6.2 Command Line Interface

All switches can perform the roles of:

- Network Operator – can view the configuration.
- Network Administrator – can perform all functions.

The user must have the proper permissions to assume the appropriate role.

6.2.1 Command Modes

The CLI has two primary command modes: EXEC and configuration. The commands available to these roles are determined by the mode the CLI is in. To access EXEC mode, enter the EXEC mode command. To access the configuration mode, enter the config terminal command when in EXEC mode.

The EXEC mode allows users to temporarily change terminal settings, perform basic tests, and display system information. Changes performed in this mode are not generally saved across system resets. The configuration mode enables features to be configured that affect the entire system.

6.2.2 Command Hierarchy

CLI commands are organized in a hierarchical manner. Commands which perform similar functions are groups together within the same level. To execute a command, start by entering the command at the top of the hierarchy.

The EXEC mode is started when a session begins on the switch. Most EXEC commands are one-time commands. The EXEC mode commands are:

- cd – change current directory
- clear – reset functions
- clock – manage the system clock
- config – enter configuration mode
- copy – copy from one file to another
- delete – delete a file
- dir – list files in a directory
- exit – exit from the EXEC
- help – displays available commands
- install – upgrade software
- move – move files
- ping – send echo messages

- reload – reboot the entire box
- run-script – run shell script
- setup – run the basic SETUP command facility
- show – show running system information
- sleep – allows sleep for a specified number of seconds
- system – system management commands
- terminal – set terminal line parameters
- write- write current configuration
- zone – execute zone server commands
- zoneset – execute zoneset commands

Configuration mode can be entered from the EXEC mode. Within the configuration mode, the configurations on the existing system can be changed. To preserve these changes, the changed configurations must be saved. From configuration mode, the interface configuration mode, zone configuration mode, and protocol-specific modes can be entered. The commands available in configuration mode are:

- clock – configure time-of-day clock
- do – EXEC command
- end – exit from configure mode to EXEC mode
- exit – exit from configure mode up one level
- fcalias – fcalias configuration commands
- fcdomain – enter the fcdomain configuration mode
- fctimer – configure fibre channel timers
- help – displays available commands
- interface – select an interface to configure
- ip – configure IP features

- logging – modify message logging facilities
- no – negate a command or set its default
- ntp – BTP configuration
- snmp-server – configure snmp server
- ssh – configure SSH parameters
- switchname – configure system's network name
- telnet – enable telnet
- username – configure user information
- zone – zone configuration commands
- zoneset – zoneset configuration commands

Also known as terminal configuration mode, configuration mode has several submodes. Each submode places the user deeper into the hierarchy.

6.3 Switch Configuration

Before configuring a switch:

- Verify physical connections
- Verify default console port parameters
- Power on the switch

The first time a fabric switch is accessed; a setup program is run which asks for the IP address and other configuration information to allow communication over the Ethernet interface.

6.3.1 Configuring the Switch

To configure a fabric switch for the first time, the following information is required:

- Administrator password
- IP address for management interface (out-of-band Ethernet interface)
- Subnet mask
- IP addresses
- SSH service (SSH key and number of key bits)
- Optional default domain name
- Optional NTP server IP address
- Optional SNMP community string
- Optional switch name

The subnet that the new switch is connected will determine the setup scenario. To manage connections from outside of the switch, the IP address must be configured. First time out-of-band access can be configured through the following general steps:

1. Power on the switch.
2. Enter administrator password.
3. Enter yes to enter the setup mode.
4. Enter yes to create additional accounts.
5. Enter yes to configure SNMP community string.
6. Enter switch name.
7. Enter yes for out-of-band management configuration.
8. Enter yes to enable Telnet service.

9. Enter no to disable the SSH service.
10. Enter no to not configure NTP server.
11. Enter noshut to configure interface to the noshut state
12. Enter deny to deny default zone policy configuration.
13. Review and edit existing configuration.
14. Enter yes to accept and save configuration.

Initial configurations can be changed later using the setup command in EXEC mode.

The switch can be accessed after the initial configuration through:

- Serial console access
- Out-of-band access

Each switch in the fabric must have a unique name which is limited to 32 alphanumeric characters.

6.3.2 Management Interface Configuration

To manage a switch, a single IP address is used by the switch management interface. Multiple, simultaneous Telnet or SNMP sessions can exist on the switch management interface.

The status of an interface can be viewed at any time using the show interface mgmt 0 command.

6.3.3 Software Upgrades

Before performing any software upgrades, the following steps should be taken:

- Review current software upgrade requirements and build recommendations based on operating environments.
- Schedule the upgrade for times when the fabric is stable.
- Verify that sufficient space is available in the volatile file system.
- Avoid power interruption during any install procedures.
- Configure the IP address for the port connection and ensure the switch has a route to the remote server.
- Retrieve an image either locally or remotely.
- Become familiar with the terminology and commands required for the upgrade.

The install all command can upgrade the entire switch. A platform validity check is performed to ensure the right image is used. If any step of the sequence fails, the step is completed and the upgrade ends. Failures can occur when:

- Sufficient space on the volatile file system is not available to access the updated image.
- A power disruption occurs when the upgrade is in progress.
- The entire path for the remote location is not specified accurately.

6.3.4 Hardware Management

The following commands can be used to manage the hardware

- Displaying the switch hardware – use the show hardware command.
- Displaying the serial number – use the show sprom mgt-module command.
- Displaying environment information – use the show environment command.

6.4 Fibre Channel Interfaces

6.4.1 Interface States

The administrative configuration of the interface and the dynamic state of the physical link determines the interface state. The states are administrative and operational. A state is either up or down. For the administrative state, up refers to an enabled interface while down refers to a disabled interface. An administrative state can disable the interface without affecting the physical link layer state change. When traffic is being transmitted or received as desired, the operational state is up. For this to be the case the interface must be administratively up, as well as the interface link layer state, and the interface initialization must be complete. When traffic cannot be transmitted or received, the interface is considered down.

When the administrative state is up and the operational state down, the reason codes are based on different nonoperational reason codes (below with their descriptions).

For all applicable modes:

- Link failure or not connected 0 the physical layer link is not operational.
- SFP not present – SFP hardware not connected.
- Initializing – physical layer link is operational and protocol initialization is in progress.
- Reconfigure fabric in progress – fabric currently being reconfigured.
- Offline – FabricWare software waiting before retrying reinitialization based on specified R_A_TOV time.
- Inactive – interface is deleted or in suspended state.
- Hardware failure – hardware failure detected.
- Error disabled – interface disabled due to error, usually because of configuration failure or incompatible buffer-to-buffer configuration.

E_Ports:

- Isolation due to ELP failure – port negotiation failed.
- Isolation due to ESC failure – port negotiation failed.
- Isolation due to domain overlap – FC domains overlapping.
- Isolation due to other side E port isolated – E-port on other end of link is isolated.
- Isolation due to invalid fabric reconfiguration – port is isolated because of fabric reconfiguration.

- Isolation due to domain manager disabled – FC domain feature is disabled.
- Isolation due to zone merge failure – zone merge operation failed.

FL_Ports:

- Nonparticipating – FL ports cannot participate in loop operations.

6.4.2 Interface Configuration

A Fibre Channel can be configured by entering configuration mode and configuring the specified interface. The command for configuring a single interface is switch(config) # interface fcl/1. To configure a range of interfaces, replace the number with a range (1 to 1-4, for example). When a FC interface is configured, a unique worldwide name (WWN) is automatically assigned. If the operational state for the interface is up, a Fibre Channel ID is assigned as well.

Interface modes consist of auto, E, F, FL, or FX port modes. To change the interface mode, enter configuration mode and identify the specific interface to change. To change the mode, use the command: switch(config-if)# switchport mode F switch(config-if)# where the mode is specified. To enable autonegotiation, use the command: switch(config-if)# switchport mode auto switch(config-if)#.

The administrative speed for an interface is automatically calculated by the switch by default. However to configure a specific speed of

1000 Mbps, 2000 Mbps, 4000 Mbps, or auto, enter configuration mode. Use the command, switch(config-if)# switchport speed 1000 switch(config-if)#, to change the speed.

The description of the interface can be changed using the command: switch(config-if)# switchport description switchname. To clear the description, use the command switch(config-if)# no switchport description.

Beacon mode enables the physical location of a specific interface to be identified through a flashing green light. By default, beacon mode is disabled on all switched. This mode has no impact on the operations of the interface. To enable beacon mode, enter configuration mode and identify the desired interface. Then use the command: switch(config-if)# switchport beacon. A flashing green light also indicates the detection of an external loopback that is causing the interfaces to be isolated. This indication will override any beacon mode configuration until after the external loopback is removed.

6.4.3 Graceful Shutdown

By default, the interfaces on a port will be shut down. A graceful shutdown can be performed when an interface in E_port mode or a port shutdown is performed by a FabricWare application. The purpose of a graceful shutdown is to shut down the interface without losing any frames. When the shutdown command is initiated, the connected switches will coordinate with each other to ensure all frames in the ports are safely sent through the link. Once this is complete, the interface is then shut down. If the Min_LS_interval interval is higher than 10 seconds, a graceful shutdown is not possible.

To shutdown an interface, enter the configuration mode and specify the interface to shut down. Use the following command to execute the shut down and disable traffic flow administratively: switch(config-if)# shutdown). To enable traffic flow, use the command: switch (config-if)# no shutdown.

6.4.4 SFP Transmitters

Acronyms are used to identify SFP hardware transmitters. These acronyms can be displayed after using the command show interface brief. If the SFP has a Cisco-assigned extended ID, the ID may be displayed rather than the transmitter type. The show interface transceiver command can be used to display both values.

The transmitter types and acronyms are:

- short wave swl
- long wave laser lwl
- long wave laser cost reduced lwcr
- electrical elec

Cisco-supported SFPs can be assigned extended transmitters including:

- CWDM-1470 c1470
- CWDM-1490 c1490

- CWDM-1510 c1510
- CWDM-1530 c1530
- CWDM-1550 c1550
- CWDM-1570 c1570
- CWDM-1590 c1590
- CWDM-1610 c1610

6.4.5 Management Interface

The switch can be configured through the management interface (mgmt0). A remote connection must be configured with the IP parameters from the CLI. This configuration allows the switch to be used. To configure the management interface, enter configuration mode and follow these steps:

1. Configure the management Ethernet interface.
2. Enter the IP address and IP subnet mask for the interface.
3. Enable the interface.
4. Return to configuration mode.
5. Configure the default gateway's IP address.
6. Return to EXEC mode.
7. Save any configuration changes.

6.5 Configuring Zones

Zones consist of multiple zone members. Members within a zone can access each other and cannot access members in different zones. Membership criteria are based on Port worldwide name. (pWWN), where pWWN is attached to the switch as a member of the zone. If zones are not used, all devices belong to a default zone. If zoning is activated and a device is not explicitly assigned to a zone, it belongs to the default zone. Devices can belong to more than one zone. Zones can be in different sizes.

Zone sets can consist of one or more zones. It can be managed as a single entity across all switches in the fabric. Zones can belong to more than one zone set. Only one zone set can be activated at a time.

Any switch connected to the fabric can be used to administrate zones. When a zone set is activated for many switch, all switches in the fabric will receive the active zone set. If a new switch is added to the existing fabric, the new switch will acquire any zone sets. Zone changes will not disrupt traffic on the fabric or ports unaffected by the change.

6.5.1 Implementation

Support for zone implementation by the Cisco MDS 9020 Fabric Switch is automatic for the following features:

- Soft-zoned name server queries
- Distribution of active zone sets only
- Access denied between unzoned devices
- Inability to change active zones without activating a full zone database
- Preservation of active zone sets across switch reboots
- Change to full database must be explicitly saved
- Existing traffic not disrupted by zone reactivation

Some zone features can be configured:

- Full zone sets can be propagated to all switches.
- Ability to change default zone for unzoned members
- Bring E ports out of isolation.

6.5.2 Configuration

Zones can be configured by assigning members in one of two ways:

- pWWN – the WWN of the N or NI port.
- FC alias – the alphabetic name associated to a WWN, and may include multiple WWN members.

Configuring a zone can be done using the following command in configuration mode: switch(config)# zone name Zone1 switch(config-zone)# where Zone 1 is the zone name. To assign a member to a specific zone, use the commands, switch(config-zone)# member <type> <value>.

To assign an alias name to a member, used the command switch(config)# fcalias name <name> switch-config-fcalias#.

6.5.3 Creating Zone Sets

Zone sets can be created with their own membership hierarchy and zone members. Access control can be specified in zones. Zone sets enforce access control in the fabric. Creating a zone with several zones includes the following steps:

1. Enter configuration mode.
2. Configure a zone set.
3. Add members to the zone.
4. Add zones to the zone set (only used if a zone must be created from a zone set prompt).

Steps 2-4 use the following commands in order:

- switch(config)# zoneset name <zoneset name> switch-config-zoneset#
- switch-config-zoneset# member <zone name>
- switch-config-zoneset# zone name <zone name> switch-config-zoneset-zone#

6.5.4 Zone Enforcement

Soft zones are a method of enforcing zoning. Each end device will discover other devices in the fabric. This discovery is done by querying the name server. When a device connects to the name server, the server will return a list of other devices that can be accessed by the device that is performing the query. Zoning restrictions apply only between the name server and the end device.

6.5.5 Link Isolation

E_ports can become isolated when two switches in the fabric are merged using an E_port and the active zone sets for each switch is different. An isolated E_port can be recovered using:

- An import from a neighboring switch's active zone set database.
- An export of the current database to the neighboring switch.
- Manual editing of the full zone set, activating the current zone set, and bringing up the link.

6.5.6 Zone Database

The zone database contains information about the current zones in the fabric. The following actions can be taken with the associated commands:

- Clearing the database – switch# clear zone database
- Renaming a zone set – switch(config)# zoneset rename oldname newname
- Renaming a zone – switch(config)# zone rename oldname newname
- Renaming z fcalias – switch(config)# fcalias rename oldname newname
- Displaying information – switch# show (zone|zoneset|zone|fcalias)

Zone databases can be merged together successfully as long as some simple rules are followed:

- Databases to be merged must be adjacent to each other.
- If either database is empty, it will be populated with the information from the other database.
- If both databases have information, zones sets can have the same name, by the zones, aliases, and attributes groups must be unique in each database, even if these components have different members.

6.6 Switch Security

The users managing a switch can be identified, granted access to, and track the actions using the authentication, authorization, and accounting (AAA) mechanism. Remote Access Dial-In User Service (RADIUS) protocols provide solutions using remote AAA servers.

Local authentication and authorization is performed using a user ID and password combination. Preshared secret keys are used to provide communication security between switches and AAA servers. These secret keys can be configured for all AAA servers or for individual AAA servers.

6.6.1 Switch Management Security

The Command Line Interface can be accessed using the console, Telnet, Secure Shell (SSH). One of more security control options can be configured, ranging from local to remote (RADIUS).

All applications using SNMP will apply normal SNMP security mechanisms. DLI security options are applied to the Cisco MDS Fabric Manager and Device Manager.

6.6.2 RADIUS

The RADIUS protocol is used to communicate with remote AAA servers. Multiple RADIUS servers can be configured, up to five. RADIUS keys are stored encrypted and in persistent storage.

The protocol is a distributed client/server protocol designed to secure networks against unauthorized access. RADIUS clients running on the switch will send authentication requests to a central RADIUS server. The central server contains all the information on user authentication and network service access.

To specify the host RADIUS server address and options, the following steps should be taken in configuration mode:

1. Specify the preshared key for the RADIUS server.
2. Specify the destination UDP port number where RADIUS authentication messages can be sent.
3. Specify the server for accounting purposes only.
4. Specify the time between retransmission to the RADIUS server.
5. Configure the number of allowed reconnect attempts.

6.6.3 AAA Services

The user names and passwords are maintained on the local system. For additional security, the password information is stored in encrypted form. Authentication is dependent on the locally stored user information. To configure local users and their roles, the username command is used. The show accounting log command will allow the local accounting log to be shown.

When the identity of the person managing the switch is going through the process of being verified, the process is called authentication. The process utilizes the user ID and password combination provided by the user to conduct the verification. Authentication can be performed either locally or remotely.

The steps for authentication follow:

1. Log into the fabric switch.
2. An authentication request is sent to the first RADIUS server.
    - If a RADIUS server fails to response, the request is sent to the next RADIUS server.
    - If all RADIUS servers fail to respond, authentication is performed through the local database.
3. If the RADIUS server finishes the authentication, the user roles are downloaded within the response.
    - If the retrieval of user roles fails, the use is assigned the network-operator role.
4. If the local database performs the authentication successfully, the use is assigned the roles configured in the local database.

6.6.4 Role-Based Authorization

Two roles are supported for authentication: network-administrator and network operator. By using role-based authorization, access to switch operations is limited by the role the user is assigned. The role defines what commands can be used, how the command can be executed, completed, or how contextual help is obtained. To display the rules associated with a specific role, use the show role command.

Every user of the fabric switch has account information that is stored on the system, including user name, user password, password expiration data, and role membership. To create or update a user account, use the command switch(config)# username <name>

password <password> expire <YYYY-MM-DD>. The show user-account command can be used to display account information.

6.6.5 Accounting Services

Information for each management session in a switch is logged to generate reports for troubleshooting and auditing purposes. The effort is consists of the accounting function of AAA and can be implemented locally or remotely using RADIUS.

To display the contents of the accounting log, use the show accounting log command.

6.6.6 SSH Services

Before enabling the Secure Shell service, use the ssh key command to generate a server key pair. The key is generated based on the SSH client version used. Each key pair can have a specified number of bits ranging from 768 to 2408. Generation of a RSA key pair for the SSH version 2 protocol requires the rsa option. A key pair is required to start a SSH session.

By default, the SSH service is disabled. To enable the service, the command, switch(config)# ssh server enable updated, should be used. Status of the SSH protocol can be obtained with the show ssh server command.

6.6.7 Administrator Password

The recovery of the administrator password requires the restoration of the factory account name password. This is performed in maintenance mode and restores the password for the Admin account name to the default (admin123). All other user accounts are removed from the switch.

The following steps are taken to reset the switch password:

1. Isolate switch from fabric.
2. Establish a serial connection from PC console port to switch console port.
3. Enter maintenance mode.
4. Enter the account name and password for maintenance mode (usually pron, prom).
5. Enter option for Reset User Accounts to Default.
6. Enter options for Reset Switch.
7. Enter yes when prompted to reset the switch.

6.6.8 Cisco Access Control Server Configuration

The Cisco Access Control Server (ACS) will utilize RADIUS protocols to provide AAA services to the environment. If a dedicated AAA server is being used already, the Cisco ACS performs user management.

6.7 SNMP Configuration

Management information between network devices is exchanged using the application layer protocol, versions SNMPv1 and SNMPv2c.

6.7.1 Communities

SNMP users are placed into communities to provide read-only and read-write access. To add or delete these communities, use the commands:

- Add read-only access: switch(config)# snmp-server community <community name> ro
- Add read-write access: switch(config)# snmp-server community <community name> rw
- Delete access: switch(config)# no snmp-server community <community name>

6.7.2 Contact Information

Each SNMP switch must have an associated contact. The information on the contact is limited to 32 characters. The snmp-server command can set the contact information and the switch location.

6.7.3 Notifications

Notifications can be sent to SNMP managers when changes occur in the switch configuration or status. These notifications can be sent as traps: system alerts generated when specified changes occur on the switch. Several configurations are available through configuration mode, as seen below:

- Enable SNMP traps – switch(config)# snmp-server enable traps
- Disable SNMP traps – switch(config)# no snmp-server enable traps
- Hosts to receive traps – switch(config)# snmp-server host <ip address> traps <snmp version> private udp-port <port #>
- Prevent host to receive traps - switch(config)# no snmp-server host <ip address> traps <snmp version> private udp-port <port #>

6.7.4 SNMP Security Information

To display configured SNMP information, use the show snmp commands. The information to be displayed must be specified in the command. The following detail information is available for display:

- SNMP User
- SNMP Community
- SNMP Host
- SNMP

6.8 Fibre Channel Routing

The standard path selection protocol used by Fibre Channel fabrics is Fabric Shortest Path First (FSPF). It is enabled by default on all FC switches. No FSPF services need to be configured unless special considerations are required. FSPF will dynamically compute routes to establish the shortest and quickest route between switches and select alternative paths in the event of failure in the original path.

6.8.1 FSPF Solutions

FSPF is used within fault tolerant fabrics using a partial or full mesh topology. In these solutions, when a particular link fails within the fabric, any switch can still communicate with all other switches in the fabric.

Redundant links replicate each connection between any pair of switches. Between a pair of switches, two or more links can be present.

When a new switch enters a fabric, a link state record (LSR) is sent to adjacent switches and then flooded throughout the fabric. The default responses for switch responses include:

- Acknowledgment Interval – the time waited for an acknowledgment from LSR before retransmission (default 5 seconds).
- Refresh Time – the time waited before sending an LSR

refresh transmission (default 30 minutes).

- Maximum Age – the time waited before dropping the LSR from the database (default 60 minutes).

6.8.2 FSPF Information

Using the show fspf command will display information about the Global FSPF, including:

- Domain number of the switch.
- Autonomous region for the switch.
- Min_LS_arrival: minimum time must elapse before the switch accepts LSR updates.
- Min_LS_interval: minimum time most elapse before the switch can transmit an LSR.
- LS_refresh_time: time lapse between refresh LSR transmissions.
- Max_age: maximum time an LSR can stay before being deleted.

The information for FSPF interfaces can be displayed with the show fspf interface command. The information displayed includes:

- Link cost
- Timer values
- Neighbors domain ID (if known)
- Local interface number
- Remote interface number (if known)

- FSPF state of the interface
- Interface counters

6.9 IP Services

6.9.1 Traffic Management

Traffic management services are performed through a console connection or the mgmt0 Ethernet interface. The management interface allows multiple simultaneous Telnet or SNMP sessions to exist. The configuration of the management interface can happen through the switch(config)# interface mgmt0 switch(config-if)#.

The IP address for the default gateway can be configured using the IP default-gateway command. The show ip route command can verify that the IP address is configured.

6.9.2 Access Control Lists

Network security is enabled through IP access control lists, which restricts IP traffic based on configured filters. A filter contains rules that are matched to an IP packet. If a match exists, the packet is permitted or dropped based on the rule. These rules can be based on protocol, address, port, ICMP type and type of service (TOS).

Protocol information is required and identifies the IP name or number. The IP can be specified as a number ranging from 0 to 255 or as the name of the protocol, such as but not limited to:

- Internet Protocol (IP)
- Transmission Control Protocol (TCP)
- User Datagram Protocol (UDP)
- Internet Control Message Protocol (ICMP)

The address information required in each filter identifies:

- Source – address of the network or host sending the packet.
- Source-wildcard – wildcard bits applied to the source.
- Destination – address of the network or host receiving the packet.
- Source-wildcard – wildcard bits applied to the destination.

Port information is optional and is specified by the number of the port ranging from – to 65535 or the name of the TCP or UDP port. Comparisons between the source and destination ports are conducted using the following options:

- Equal – eq
- Greater than – gt
- Less than – lt
- Range or ports - range

The most common UDP and TFCP port numbers are:

- UDP 53 DNS

- UDP 69 TFTP
- UDP 123 NTP
- UDP 161 SNMP
- UDP 162 SNMP-TRAP
- UDP 514 Syslog
- UDP 1645/1812 RADIUS authentication
- UDP 1646/1813 RADIUS accounting
- TCP 20 FTP
- TCP 21 FTP-Data
- TCP 22 SSH
- TCP 23 Telnet
- TCP 25 SMTP
- TCP 65 TACACS-DS
- TCP 80 WWW
- TCP 115 SFTP
- TCP 143 HTTP
- TCP 5988 WBEM-HTTP
- TCP 5989 WBEM-HTTPS

ICMP configurations can identify type or code using a range from – to 255. The value for each ICMP type is:

- Echo 8
- Echo-reply 0
- Destination unreachable 3
- Traceroute 30
- Time exceeded 11

All ICMP redirect packets are rejected.

The TOS information that can be used to filter IP packets can be in the form of TOS level or TOS name. The TOS level can be expressed as a number ranging from 0 to 15. The TSO name can be:

- Max-reliability
- Max-throughput
- Min-delay
- Min-monetary-cost
- Normal

To create an IP-ACL, a filter name and one or more access condition(s) need to be specified. The source and destination address must match the condition. The filter is then applied to the specified interfaces. The command for creating an access list is switch(config)# ip access-list.

Some of the actions that can be done to an access list are:

- Permitting specific types of traffic
- Denying specific types of traffic
- Permitting traffic from a specific network
- Denying traffic from a specific network
- Adding filters to the end of the ACL
- Removing entries from an ACL
- Reading the ACL Log Dump

6.9.3 ACL Interface Application

ACLs can be defined without applying them and have no effect on the interface until they are. ACLs should be applied to interfaces closest to the traffic source. They can be applied as inbound filters or outbound filters.

Access-group options control access to the interface. Only one access filter can be applied to each interface in each direction. A different ACL can be applied to the ingress and egress directions of traffic through a switch. An access group will be active when it is created. To create an access group, use the switch (config)# ip access-group command.

To see the contents of configured access filters, use the show ip access-list command.

6.10 Domain Parameters

6.10.1 Domain Phases

Within the Fibre Channel domain, the following actions are performed in phases:

- Principle switch selection
- Domain ID distribution
- FC ID allocation

- Fabric reconfiguration

6.10.2 Domain Restart

FC domains are started either disruptively or nondisruptively. A disruptive restart will send frames for the reconfigured fabric (RCF) to other switches in the fabric. In a nondisruptive restarts sends build fabric (BD) frames to other switches in the fabric.

Most configurations are applied to their corresponding runtime values. To apply changes to the runtime settings, use the fcdomain restart command. Use the restart disruptive option to apply most of the configurations to their runtime values.

6.10.3 Domain Configuration

The domain ID can be static or preferred. By default, the configuration domain is 0 with a configured type of preferred. When a subordinate switch requests a domain, the process that follows is:
A configured domain IP request is sent to the principal switch.
The principal switch assigned the requested domain ID.
If the request domain ID is unavailable, another ID is assigned

6.11 System Message Logging

System message logging provides information for controlling logging for monitoring and troubleshooting, defining the types of captured logging information and the destination server where captured logging information should be forwarded. The switch will by default log all normal but significant system messages to a log file and send those messages to the system console. The system messages to be saved can be defined based on type of facility and severity. Each message is time-stamped to enhance real-time debugging and management.

Logged system messages can be accessed using the CLI or they can be saved to a properly configured system message logging server. Up to 1200 entries can be saved by the switch software. Messages can be access remotely through Telnet, SSH, or the console port or by viewing the logs on the system message logging server. Logs can be displayed using the show logging logfile command.

6.11.1 Logging Facilities

The internal logging facilities that can be configured for logging are:

- all All facilities
- auth Authorization systems
- fcdomain FC domain
- fcns Nameserver

- fcs FCS
- fspf FSPF
- ipconf IP configuraiton
- module Switching module
- ntp NTP
- port Port
- sysmgr System manager
- user User process
- zone Zone server

External logging facilities include:

- auth Authorization system
- authpriv Private authorization system
- cron cron or at facility
- daemon System daemons
- ftp File transfer Protocol
- kernel Kernel
- local0 to local7 Locally defined messages
- lpr Line printer system
- mail Mail system
- news USENET news
- syslog Internal system messages
- user User processor
- uucp UNIX-to-UNIC Copy Program

6.11.2 Severity Levels

The severity levels supported by system message logs are (keyword, level, description):

- Emergency 0 System unusable
- Alerts 1 Immediate action required
- Critical 2 Critical conditions
- Errors 3 Error conditions
- Warnings 4 Warning conditions
- Notifications 5 Normal but significant condition
- Informational 6 Informational message only
- Debugging 7 Debugging messages

A logging facility can have a configured severity level by using the switch(config)# logging level <facilities> <level>

6.11.3 Logging Information

The show logging command can be used to display the current system message logging configuration. Other display options for the show logging command include:

- Log file
- Logging facility and severity
- Logging information
- Last few lines of log file
- Monitor logging states

- Server information

6.11.4 System Processes

The show processes command can be used to display general information about all the processes being executed on the switch. Default information includes:

- PID – process ID
- PPID – aren't process identification number
- %CPU – CPU utilization for last one second
- TIME ELAPSED – elapsed time
- COMMAND – process name

The command can be used to display process log information or details for all processes.

6.11.5 System Status

The show system command can be used to display system-related status information. With this command system reset information and uptime can be displayed.

6.12 Commands

Below are the common commands found in Cisco managed Fibre Channels:

To change the default file system:

cd [bootflash: |volatile]

where bootflash: the flash image of a non-volatile file system

volatile: the flash image of a volatile file system

To clear interface counters:

clear counters interface {all | fc 1/port}

where all clears all interface counters

fc Fibre Channel interface to clear counters

1/port specifies slot q and the port numbers from 1 to 20

To clear fspf counters:

clear fspf counters [interface fc 1/port]

where interface fc Fibre Channel interface to clear counters (optional)

1/port specifies slot q and the port numbers from 1 to 20

To clear ip access-list counters:

clear ip access-list counters *list-name*

where *list-name* specifies the IP access list name

To clear zone database:

clear zone database

To set the time zone and summer-time-of-day:

clock {summer-time *daylight-timezone-name start-week start-day start-month start-time end-week end-day end-month end-time daylight-offset-to-be-added-in-minutes* | time zone *timezone-name hours-offset minutes-offset*}

To change the system time:

clock set *HH:MM:SS DD Month YYYY*

To enter configuration mode:

config terminal

To save a backup of the system software:

copy *source destination*

where source location or name of source file to be copied

destination location or name of copied file

To delete a file:

delete [bootflash:*filename* |volatile:*filename*]

where bootflash: the flash image of a non-volatile file system

volatile: the flash image of a volatile file system

filename the name of the file to be deleted

To display the contents of a file system:

dir [bootflash:*filename* |volatile:*filename*]

where bootflash: the flash image of a non-volatile file system

volatile: the flash image of a volatile file system

filename the name of the file to be deleted

To execute an EXEC mode command:

do *command*

where *command* the EXEC command to be executed

To exit any configuration mode and return to EXEC mode:

end

To exit any configuration mode or close an active terminal session and terminate the EXEC:

exit

To configure an FC alias (the second line is the member subcommand):

fcalias name *alias-name*

member pwwn *pwwn-id*

where *alias-name* name of the fcalias

member adds a member to the fcalias

pwwn *pwwn-id*adds a member using the port WWN

To rename an FC alias:

fcalias rename *current-name new-name*

where current-name the current name of the fcalias

new-name the new name of the fcalias

To configure the Fibre Channel domain:

fcdomain {domain *id* {preferred | static} priority *value* | restart [disruptive]}

where domain id configures the domain ID and type

preferred sets the domain ID as preferred

static sets the domain ID as static

priority *value* specifies the FC domain

priority

restart restarts a disruptive or nondisruptive reconfiguration

disruptive forces a disruptive fabric reconfiguration

To change the default Fibre Channel timers:

fctimer {d_s_tov *milliseconds* | e_d_tov *milliseconds* | r_a_tov *milliseconds*}

where d_s_tov *milliseconds* the distributed services time out value

e_d_tov *milliseconds* the error detect time out value

r_a_tov *milliseconds* the resolution allocation time out value

To configure the FSPF link cost for an interface:

fspf cost *link-cost*

where *link-cost* ranges from 1 to 65,535

To set the maximum interval before a hello message is considered lost:

fspf dead-interval *seconds*

To verify the health of the link:

fspf hello-interval *seconds*

To specify the time waited before an unacknowledged link state update should be transmitted on the interface:

fspf retransmit-interval *seconds*

To upgrade firmware on the switch:

install all system volatile:filename

where system upgrades the system image

volatile: the volatile file system

filename source file to be installed

To configure management interface on a switch:

interface mgmt 0

To create an access group to use an access list:

ip access-group *group-name* [in | out]

where *group-name* defines the IP access-group name

in specifies group for ingress traffic

out specifies group for egress traffic

To configure IP access control lists:

ip access-list *list-name* {deny | permit} *ip-protocol*
{*src-addr src-wildcard*}
{*dest-addr dest-wildcard* |*operator port-value*}
[*operator*port *port-value*]
[established |icmp-type *icmp-value*]
[tos *tos-value*]

where *list-name* identifies the ACL

deny denies access

permit provides access

ip-protocol name or # of IP protocol

src-addr source network address

src-wildcard source wildcard bits

dest-addr destination network

address

dest-wildcard destination wildcard bits

operator compares source and

destination ports

port *port-value* decimalnumber of name

ofTCP or UDP port

icmp-type *icmp-value* filters ICMP

packets by message type

established established connection

tos tos-value type of service

To assign an IP address to an Ethernet management port:

ip address *address netmask*

To configure the IP address of a default gateway:

ip default-gateway *destination-ip-address*

To modify the message logging facilities:

logging level all *severity-level*

To set monitor message logging:

logging monitor *severity-level*

To set the IP address of the remote message logging server:

no logging server *ip address*

To move a file to another filename:

move *source destination*

To configure a Network Time Protocol (NTP) server:

ntp server *ip-address*

To diagnose basic network connectivity:

ping i*p-address*

To configure RADIUS server:

radius-server host {*server-name* | *ip-address*} [key *shared-secret*] [accounting] [auth-port *port-number*] [authentication] [retransmit *count*] [timeout seconds [retransmit *count*]]

where *server-name* the RADIUS server DNS name

ip-address the RADIUS server IP address

auth-port *port-number* configures server port

authentication use for authentication

accounting use for accounting

key shared key

shared-secret configures preshared key

retransmit *count* # of times connection is tried

timeout *seconds* time between transmissions

To reload the switch:

reload

To execute the commands within a file:

run-script [filename | running-config | startup-config | volatile:filename | bootflash:filename]

where bootflash: the flash image of a non-volatile file system

volatile: the flash image of a volatile file system

filename the name of the file to be deleted

running-config configuration currently running

startup-config configuration used during startup

To enter a switch setup mode:

setup

Various display commands:

show accounting log

show accounting logsize

show clock

show environment [power | temperature]

show fcalias [name *fcalias-name*]

show fcdomain [domain-list]

show fcns database [detail|domain *domain-id*|fcid *fcid-id*]

show fcs database

show fctimer [d_s_tov|e_d_tov|r_a_tov]

show fdmi database [detail]

show flogi database

show fspf [interface]

show hardware

show interface {[brief]|counters [brief]|description|fc 1/port [brief] |mgmt 0 | transceiver}

show ip access-list [*list-name* | usage]

show ip route

show logging [info | last *lines* | level | logfile | monitor | server]

show module [uptime]

show processes {log [details]}

show radius-server

show running-config [diff]

show snmp [community | host | user]

show sprom mgmt-module

show ssh server

show startup-config

show switchname

show system [reset-reason | uptime]

show tech-support [brief | create |details | interface | module 1]

show telnet server

show terminal

show user-account

show users

show version

show zone [active | member {fcalias *alias-name* | pwwn *wwn* } | name *string* | status]

show zoneset [active | name *zoneset-name*]

To disable an interface:

shutdown [force]

To delay an action for a specified number of seconds:

sleep *seconds*

To configure the SNMP server information:

snmp-server [community *string* [ro|rw] | contact [*name*] | enable traps | location [*location*]]

where community *string*	defines the SNMP community string
ro	sets read-only access
rw	sets read-write access
contact	configures system contact
name	name of contact
enable traps	enables SNMP traps
location	configures system location
location	defines system location

To configure the destination host of an SNMP notification operation:

snmp-server host host-address traps version [1 } 2c] community-strings [udp-port port]

where host-address name of IP address of host

traps sends SNMP traps to host

version version of SNMP

1 SNMPv1

2c SNMPv2c

community-string sends password like string

udp-port defines the port UDP port

port UDP port number

To generate an SSH key:

ssh key rsa [*bits*]

To enable an SSH server:

ssh server enable

To change the name of the switch:

switchname *name*

To enable Telnet servers:

telnet server enable

To configure attributes for the terminal:

terminal [length *lines* | session-timeout *minutes*]

where length lines defines the number of lines on the screen

session-timeout defines the session timeout value

To define a user:

username *name* [password *user-password* | [expire *days*] | role *rolename*]

where *name* defines the name of user

password configures user password

user-password defines password

expire *days* defines expire date

role role name of user

rolename role name

To clear the startup configuration:

write erase [boot]

To define whether a default zone permits access to everything in the default zone:

zone default-zone [permit]

To create a zone:

zone name *zone-name*

To rename a zone:

zone rename *current-name new-name*

To group zones under one zone set:

zoneset [name zoneset-name| activate name zoneset-name | distribute full | rename current-name new name]

where name *zoneset-name* creates zone set

activate *zoneset-name* activate a zone set

distribute full enables full zone set propagation

member *zone-name* defines the existing zone

rename rename a zone set

current-name current zone set name

new-name new zone set name

7 *Practice Exam*

7.1 Refresher Questions”

The following multiple-choice questions are a refresher.

Question 1

Which of the network topologies are the simplest implementations of a Fibre Channel network?

A) Bus
B) Arbitrated Loop
C) Point-to-point
D) Switched Fabric

Question 2

Which of the following is not a category for SCSI commands?

A) Reading
B) Writing
C) Bidirectional
D) Control

Question 3

Which of the following iSNS component is responsible for initiating State Change Notifications?

A) Servers
B) Clients
C) Database
D) Protocol

Question 4

Which of the following IP addresses is a private address?

A) 172.24.98.168
B) 193.168.25.10
C) 14.32.168.172
D) 201.172.101.214

Question 5

What is the technique used to emulate a system for better performance?

A) Zoning
B) Optimization
C) Virtualization

D) All of the above

Question 6

Which of the following is a form of asymmetric encryption?

A) RC4
B) RSA
C) AES
D) DES

Question 7

Which of the following features is used to ensure in-order exchange of frames across the network?

A) FSPF
B) Latency
C) QoS
D) Trunking

Question 8

Which of the following is not a task of a SAN management system?

A) Prediction
B) Design

C) Failure Notification
D) Prevention

Question 9

Which of the following is not part of the physical layer of the Fibre Channel?

A) Physical Interface/Media
B) Signaling Protocol
C) Transmission Protocol
D) Protocol Mapping Layer

Question 10

Which of the following CLI commands should be used to exit from the current configuration mode to return to EXEC mode?

A) end
B) exit
C) shutdown
D) all of the above

Question 11

Ordered sets are a function of which FC layer?

A) FC-4
B) FC-3
C) FC-2
D) FC-1

Question 12

How many concurrent clients can be supported by a single instance of Fabric Manager Server?

A) 8
B) 16
C) 128
D) 1024

Question 13

When a system is first introduced to the network and a backup is performed; what type of backup will be executed?

A) Differential incremental
B) Cumulative incremental
C) Full backup
D) Any of the above

Question 14

When data traveling through the fabric doesn't reach its destination because a port is impacted by the traffic, what is the term used to describe the situation?

A) Blocking
B) Congestion
C) Disconnect
D) Any of the above

Question 15

Validation of the user's identity is performed by what system of the access control architecture?

A) Host
B) Requester
C) Authenticator
D) All of the Above

Question 16

In designing a Storage Area Network, which of the following is a factor impacted by the distance between devices?

A) Bandwidth

B) Latency
C) Integrity
D) Management

Question 17

What is the subnetwork for IP address 234.34.192.102 and subnet mask 255.255.25.0

A) 234.34.0.0
B) 234.34.25.0
C) 234.34.192.0
D) 234.34.67.0

Question 18

Discovery Domains are a service provided by which protocol

A) IP
B) iFCP
C) IPFC
D) iSNS

Question 19

Which of the following port classes is commonly found between two fibre channel switches to form an inter-switch link that allows for routing Virtual SANs?

A) TE_port
B) EX_port
C) E_port
D) F_port

Question 20

How many layers are in the Fibre Channel protocol?

A) 4
B) 5
C) 8
D) Same as OSI model

Question 21

How many bits in length is the Logical Unit Number?

A) 8
B) 32
C) 64
D) 128

Question 22

What class does the IP address 198.52.5.214 belong?

A) Class A
B) Class B
C) Class C
D) Class D

Question 23

Fibre Channel over IP was developed by what organization?

A) Cisco
B) Internet Engineering Task Force
C) American National Standards Institute
D) International Business Machines

Question 24

Redundant Arrays of Inexpensive Disks are an example of what level of virtualization?

A) Storage Subsystem
B) Fabric
C) Server
D) File System

Question 25

What is the technique used to expand the fabric using ISLS to interconnecting switches and directors?

A) Trunking
B) Cascading
C) Virtualizing
D) Oversubscription

Question 26

When multiple copies of the same data can be found in different locations, what is the storage approach being used?

A) Centralized
B) Virtualization
C) Replication
D) Distributed

Question 27

What layer of storage management is zoning?

A) Network Management
B) Resource Management
C) Data Management

D) Element Management

Question 28

What component of the Fabric Manager allows switch events of the fabric to be monitored from a remote location?

A) Traffic Analyzer
B) Performance Manager
C) Web Client
D) Server

Question 29

What protocol is used in out-band management of the fabric to communicate necessary information?

A) IP
B) RADIUS
C) CLI
D) SNMP

Question 30

Which of the following severity levels support system message logs requiring immediate action?

A) Alerts
B) Emergency
C) Critical
D) Warnings

Question 31

Which class of Fibre Channel service provides buffer-to-buffer flow control?

A) Class 2
B) Class 3
C) Class 4
D) Class 6

Question 32

Which of the following layers is responsible for providing the Open Fibre Control (OFC) system?

A) FC-0
B) FC-2
C) FC-3
D) FC-1

Question 33

The SES protocol is used within what layer of Storage Management?

A) Application Management
B) Data Management
C) Resource Management
D) Element Management

Question 34

Which of the following RAID levels does not provide any redundancy in storage?

A) RAID 0
B) RAID 1
C) RAID 3
D) RAID 5

Question 35

The size of the fabric is limited by what component?

A) Hop count
B) Distance
C) Switch type
D) Congestion

Question 36

What technique can be used to support multiple operating platforms by segregating the storage network into isolated parts?

A) Virtualization
B) Segregation
C) Access Security
D) Zoning

Question 37

Which of the following protocols is a FC layer 4 protocol for mapping IBM's channel-to-control-using cabling infrastructure?

A) IFCP
B) FICON
C) FCIP
D) FCP

Question 38

Which of the following is not a type of IPv6 address?

A) Unicast
B) Anycast
C) Broadcast

D) Multicast

Question 39

Which of the following is not a protocol layer of SCSI?

A) Arbitration
B) Status Out
C) Message In
D) Selection

Question 40

Which class of port is generally found on the switch port of an arbitrated loop?

A) F_port
B) NL_port
C) N_port
D) FL_port

8 Answer Guide

8.1 Answers to Questions

Question 1

Answer: C

Reasoning: The simplest network topology for Fibre Channel is a point-to-point. A point-to-point topologies is considered a bus topology but bus is not within the vocabulary of FC as it relates to topology. Arbitrated loops and switched fabric topologies are more advanced topologies used.

Question 2

Answer: D

Reasoning: Categories for SCSI commands are N, W, R, and B (non-data, writing, reading, bidirectional).

Question 3

Answer: A

Reasoning: Servers are responsible for initiating State Change Notification as well as storing information in the iSNS database and responding to queries made by iSNS clients.

Question 4

Answer: A

Reasoning: Class B private addresses range from 172.16.0.0 to 172.31.255.255.

Question 5

Answer: C

Reasoning: Virtualization is a technique for emulation, partitioning and combining resources. One of the benefits is better performance.

Question 6

Answer: B

Reasoning: RSA is a form of asymmetric encryption. The remaining choices are symmetric encryption solutions.

Question 7

Answer: D

Reasoning: Trunking enables traffic to be distributed across an ILS while preserving the order of frames.

Question 8

Answer: B

Reasoning: Though SAN management may lead to design activities for improvement or new technologies, design is not a task of the system.

Question 9

Answer: D

Reasoning: Protocol Mapping Layer is part of the upper layer of the Fibre Channel, along with Common Services.

Question 10

Answer: A

Reasoning: The command, end, is used in configuration mode to return to EXEC mode. Exit is used to go up one level, while shutdown will close out the session.

Question 11

Answer: C

Reasoning: FC-1, or Signaling Protocol layer, defines ordered sets.

Question 12

Answer: B

Reasoning: 16 concurrent clients can be supported by a single Fabric Manager.

Question 13

Answer: C

Reasoning: All backup solutions require the first backup to be a full backup.

Question 14

Answer: A

Reasoning: Blocking stops data from reaching its destination, while congestion slows it down.

Question 15

Answer: C

Reasoning: In an access control system, the authenticator is responsible for validating the user's identity.

Question 16

Answer: B

Reasoning: Distance will always proportionally impact latency.

Question 17

Answer: A

Reasoning: 234.24.0.0 is the determined subnetwork.

Question 18

Answer: D

Reasoning: Discovery Domains are a service of iSNS which divides storage nodes into management groups.

Question 19

Answer: A

Reasoning: E_ports are used to connect two FC switches to create an ISL. Extended ISL connections to allow Virtual SANs are supported by Cisco standard TE_port.

Question 20

Answer: B

Reasoning: The protocol works similar in operation to the OSI model; but instead of 8 layers, there are five layers (physical, data link, network, common services, Protocol Mapping).

Question 21

Answer: C

Reasoning: The LUN is 64 bits in length.

Question 22

Answer: C

Reasoning: Class C addresses range from 192.0.1.0 to 233.255.255.0.

Question 23

Answer: B

Reasoning: FCIP is a technology developed by IETF (Internet Engineering Task Force).

Question 24

Answer: A

Reasoning: RAID is an example of virtualization at the storage subsystem level.

Question 25

Answer: B

Reasoning: Cascading provides a seamless extension of the fabric.

Question 26

Answer: D

Reasoning: Two approaches are available for storing data: distributed and centralized. When multiple copies of the same data can be found, and distributed approach is being used.

Question 27

Answer: A

Reasoning: Network management focuses on the mapping of physical components of the SAN network. Zoning is a method performed by network management.

Question 28

Answer: C

Reasoning: Remote monitoring of switch events, performance, and inventory is available through the Fabric Manager Web Client.

Question 29

Answer: D

Reasoning: SNMP is the protocol used to fabric management systems to communicate information out-of-band.

Question 30

Answer: A

Reasoning: Alerts, severity 1, require immediate action. Some may say emergency, severity 0, would also require immediate action, but the severity shows when the system is unusable.

Question 31

Answer: B

Reasoning: Class 3 systems provides buffer-to-buffer flow control to the fabric.

Question 32

Answer: A

Reasoning: The OFC system is a safety system provided in the Physical Interface/Media layer, or FC-0.

Question 33

Answer: D

Reasoning: Element Management uses SCSI Enclosure Services (SES) to generate topology information.

Question 34

Answer: A

Reasoning: RAID 0 performs a simple level of disk striping and does not have any redundancy in the drives.

Question 35

Answer: A

Reasoning: The most precise answer is hop count for limiting the size of the fabric. Several hops can be contained in the same geographical distance as a single hop, but from a network perspective, the multiple hops are the longer distance.

Question 36

Answer: D

Reasoning: Zoning is the correct answer as a technique for segregating the network. Efforts can be used to support multiple platforms, organization groups, or individuals. Zoning can be physical or logical through virtualization.

Question 37

Answer: B

Reasoning: FICON, or Fibre Connectivity, maps IBM's ESCON to standard FC services and infrastructures.

Question 38

Answer: C

Reasoning: IPv6 does not have a classification for a broadcast address.

Question 39

Answer: B

Reasoning: There are 9 layers, or SCSI bus phases. They are BUS FREE, ARBITRATION, SELECTION, MESSAGE OUT, COMMAND OUT, DATA OUT/IN, STATUS IN, MESSAGE IN, RESELECTION. Status out is not a bus phase.

Question 40

Answer: D

Reasoning: Understanding port notations is simple. Ports connections on nodes or hosts are denoted by an 'N.' Port connections on switches are denoted by a 'F.' If the connections are to an arbitrated loop, an 'L' is added, while no extra notation defines a connection to a point-to-point topology. Given these guidelines, a port connection from a switch to an arbitrated loop would be denoted as 'FL_port.'

9 References

Meyers, Mike. *CompTIA A+ PC Technician*, McGraw-Hill, Chicago: 2007.

CompTIA Network+ ExamObjectives. Computing Technology Industry Association: 2008.

Tipton, Harold F. and Henry, Kevin. *Official (ISC)2 Guide to the CISSP CBK.* Auerbach Publications, Boca Raton: 2007.

Lammle, Todd. *CCNA INTRO Introduction of Cisco Networking Technologies Study Guide.* Wiley Publishing, Inc. Indianapolis, Indiana: 2006.

Odom, Wendell CCIE; Healy, Rus CCIE; and Mehta Naren CCIE, *CCIE Routing and Switching Exam Certification Guide Third Edition.* Cisco Press, Indianapolis, Indiana: 2008.

McGregor, Mark. *Cisco CCIE Fundamentals: Network Design and Case Studies.* Cisco Press: 1998

Tate, Jon; Lucchese, Fabiano; and Moore, Richard. I*ntroduction to Storage Area Networks.* IBM: July 2006

Special Edition: Using Storage Area Networks, Que: 2002

Cisco Fabric Manager Fundamentals Configuration Guide, Cisco Systems, Inc.: 2009.

Websites

www.artofservice.com.au

www.theartofservice.org

www.theartofservice.com

10 *Index*

A

access control 4, 46, 114
Access Control Server (ACS) 6, 121
AES (Advanced Encryption Standard) 4, 50, 54-5, 152
ANSI (American National Standards Institute) 12, 81, 94, 158
applications 4, 36, 40-1, 46-7, 59-60, 68, 73-4, 76, 87-9, 92, 94, 98, 117
arbitrated loop 13-14, 38-9, 83, 150, 164, 172
authentication 49, 61, 98, 116, 118-19, 143
authorization 43, 98, 116-17
availability 36, 46, 76, 84, 92

B

backups 5, 70-2, 74, 76, 137, 154, 167
bandwidth 36, 43, 65, 86-9, 155
bits 16, 21, 23, 25, 27-8, 52-3, 55, 83-4, 147, 157, 169

C

Cascading 4, 63, 159, 169
change 13, 24, 75, 99-100, 108-9, 112-13, 136-7, 140, 147
CIDR (Classless Interdomain Routing) 3, 21, 27-8
Cisco 9, 91, 94, 136, 158, 168
classifications 84, 172
CLI (command-Line interface) 97-9, 111, 132, 160
Command Line Interface 5, 98-9, 117
commands 7, 15, 98-102, 104-5, 108-10, 114, 119-20, 122-3, 129, 135-6, 138, 144, 167, 172
components 18, 33, 64, 68, 74, 77, 116, 160, 162
computers 20, 27-9, 56, 58, 78
confidentiality 49, 51
configurations 5-6, 18, 23, 39, 67, 91, 95-6, 98-9, 101, 104, 111, 113, 123, 126, 131
congestion 32, 65, 155, 162
connections 14, 38-9, 43-4, 58, 60-2, 68, 82, 87, 90, 103, 124, 143, 172

contact 10, 122, 146
copy 26, 51, 100
cost 4, 36, 40, 43, 45, 64, 66-7, 70, 92
counters 53, 136, 145
CRC (Cyclic Redundancy Check) 85
credentials 79-80

D

Data Encryption Standard 4, 52
data management 75-6, 159, 162
data security 4, 45, 49, 70
database 64, 113, 115-16, 125, 151
decrypt 50-1, 54
delivery 20, 23, 88-9
design 36-7, 54, 91, 152, 166
Discovery Domain (DD) 19, 156, 168
display 98-9, 110, 119-20, 123, 134-5, 138
distance 39-40, 155, 162, 168, 171
distribute 59, 149
domains 92, 107, 131

E

emulation 40, 166
encoding 82
encryption 4, 50, 52, 54-6, 61
entities 8, 12, 57-9, 93
environments 10, 48, 67, 83, 92, 94, 121, 144
exams 9-10
exchange 56, 85
EXEC 99-100, 138

F

Fabric Manager 77-80, 97, 160
fabric switch 94, 96, 102-3, 113, 119
facilities 132-4
failure 13, 38-9, 41, 68, 124
FCAP (Fibre Channel Authentication Protocol) 93
FCIP (Fibre Channel over IP) 3, 32-3, 158, 163, 169

FCP (Fibre Channel Protocol) 12, 86, 163
Fibre Channel 3, 5, 12-13, 18, 32-3, 39, 66, 77, 81, 83, 86-9, 92, 95, 108, 157-8, 165-6
file system 45, 136, 138, 144, 158
filter 126-7, 129
FL 14, 108, 164, 172
flash image 136, 138, 144
formula 25, 55
frames 33, 62-3, 65-6, 84-9, 91, 109, 131, 152, 166
FSPF (fabric shortest path first) 4, 62, 64, 124, 152
functions 28, 76, 86, 99-100, 153

G

groups 28, 45, 86, 100, 141

H

hardware 17, 36, 38, 94, 106, 145
hierarchy 57, 100, 102
hubs 13, 39, 65

I

identification 47-8
implementation 6, 35, 37, 67, 74-5, 92, 96, 113, 150
in-band 43-4, 76-7
incremental backups 5, 71-2
individuals 10, 45, 48, 171
information 8, 19, 33, 37, 48-9, 58, 75, 77, 80, 83-5, 103, 115-17, 120, 122-3, 125, 132
infrastructure 33, 75, 92, 172
initiators 15, 17, 19, 64
input 43, 53, 55
integer 26, 56
interconnects 39, 67, 75, 77
interface 15, 23, 47, 78, 81, 101, 104, 106-11, 129-30, 140-1, 145-6
Internet 22-3, 28-32, 62
IP (Internet Protocol) 3, 17, 20, 24, 27-8, 30, 32, 81, 86, 97-8, 126-7, 151, 156, 158, 160
ISLs (inter-switch link) 14, 62-6, 79, 90, 92, 156, 168

K

key 50-2, 54-5, 62, 120, 143
key pair 51, 57, 120

L

Latency 4, 40, 65, 152, 156
layers 13, 16, 41, 76-7, 81-3, 157, 159, 161-2, 168, 172
liability 8
limitations 19, 92
links 2, 64, 82, 84-6, 107, 110, 115, 124, 140
location 43, 70, 73, 76, 146, 159
logging 132, 145
logs 2, 61, 119, 132, 145, 160
LUNs (Logical Unit Number) 3, 16, 42, 46, 95, 157, 169

M

management 18, 32, 36, 40-1, 43, 68, 76, 90, 132, 156
management interface 6, 98, 103, 111, 126
mask 24-8
members 94-5, 112, 114, 116, 139, 146
message 29, 50-1, 53, 55, 61, 88, 132, 140, 164, 172
modes 52, 54, 74, 87, 99-101, 108-9
modifications 71-2
module 58, 145
monitor 67, 76, 78-9, 99, 145

N

network 12-13, 20, 23-9, 35, 37, 40, 59-60, 72-3, 76-7, 86, 92-3, 117, 127, 152, 154, 168
network management 74, 76, 98, 159, 170
Network Time Protocol (NTP) 97, 128, 143
nodes 13-14, 23, 86, 172
notifications 6, 19, 90, 122-3
NTP (Network Time Protocol) 97, 128, 143
number 19-20, 22, 25-8, 39, 55, 67, 82, 101, 103, 108, 118, 120, 127, 146-8

O

operating systems 37, 41-2, 46, 63, 92, 95, 97
organizations 28-31, 35, 59, 70, 82, 158

P

packet 20, 23, 30-1, 126-7, 142
passwords 47-8, 61, 79, 98, 118, 120-1, 147
PAT (Port Address Translation) 3, 30-1
paths 43, 64, 66, 105, 124
performance 36, 69-71, 73, 76, 79, 99, 151, 166, 170
person 8, 45, 47, 49, 51, 59, 118
PKI (Public Key Infrastructures) 4, 57, 59
ports 12-14, 31, 38, 62-6, 82, 84-8, 90-1, 107-10, 112-13, 115, 123, 126-7, 136, 157, 164, 168
power 63, 67, 97, 103, 144
privacy 45, 61
private key 50-1, 56, 59
problems 24, 27, 35-6, 39, 91
process 16, 33, 48-9, 51, 54, 57-8, 70, 73, 75, 89, 118, 131, 135, 145
Protocol Mapping Layer 13, 81, 153, 166
protocols 15, 18, 20, 32-3, 57, 61, 64, 77, 85-6, 91, 116-17, 120, 126-7, 151, 156, 163

Q

queries 19, 80, 115, 165

R

RADIUS (Remote Access Dial-In User Service) 6, 116-17, 120, 160
RAID (Redundant Array of Inexpensive Disks) 68-70, 162, 169, 171
range 20-1, 108, 127-8, 166, 169
Reasoning 165-72
receiver 50-1, 61
redundancy 69-70, 162, 171
replication 73-4, 159
requirements 35-7, 74

resources 36, 40-2, 48, 67-8, 76, 95, 166
roles 47-8, 97-9, 118-19
routing 14, 22, 28, 157
RSA 51, 55, 61, 152, 166
rules 84, 116, 119, 126

S

SAN 4, 32, 35-6, 38-9, 42, 45-6, 49, 65-7, 70-1, 73-6, 93
scalability 19, 44, 94
SCSI (Small Computer System Interface) 14-15, 81, 88, 164
Secure Sockets Layer (SSL) 60
security 4, 36, 45-6, 49-50, 60, 91, 94-5, 118
servers 18, 38-9, 42-3, 58-9, 72-3, 75, 97-8, 115, 117-18, 143, 145, 151, 158, 160, 165
services 8, 19, 32, 46-7, 86, 90, 97, 120, 126, 142, 156, 168
SES (SCSI Enclosure Services) 77, 171
shutdown 110, 146, 153, 167
signal 74, 84
SNMP (Simple Network Management Protocol) 78, 97-8, 117, 128, 147, 160, 170
software 17, 38, 41, 91, 94
solutions 35-7, 41, 43, 45-6, 54, 72-3, 116, 124
source 31, 82, 127, 129, 142
SSH (Secure Shell) 4, 61, 97, 117, 120, 128, 132
steps 37, 103, 105, 111, 114, 118-19, 121
storage 4, 35-8, 40, 42, 44, 65, 67, 69, 75, 95, 162
Storage Area Networks 12, 35, 155, 173
storage devices 18-19, 65, 68, 75, 95
storage management 43-4, 74, 159, 162
subnet 24-7, 103
subnetworks 24-5, 28, 156
switch 6, 14, 20, 33, 62-6, 77-8, 90-3, 95, 97-100, 102-5, 108-18, 120-6, 129-32, 134-5, 141, 172
system 39, 46-9, 57, 68, 82, 88-90, 96, 100-1, 119, 134, 136, 138, 141, 144-5, 154-5, 170

T

technique 45, 151, 159, 163, 166, 171
technologies 12, 32, 36, 57, 68-9, 74, 81-2, 94, 166, 169

Telnet 61, 97, 117, 128, 132
time 16, 19, 30, 41, 53, 65, 71, 75, 83, 85, 102-4, 112, 118, 124-5, 140
topologies 3, 12, 38-9, 64, 75, 165
traffic 62-3, 66, 79, 91, 94, 106, 113, 129-30, 155, 166
Transmission Control Protocol (TCP) 20, 60, 127
traps 123, 146-7
Trunking 4, 66, 92, 152, 159, 166
trust 47, 57, 59, 93

U

UDP (User Datagram Protocol) 60, 127
upgrade 67, 105, 141
user 45, 47-9, 56, 62, 98-9, 102, 116-19, 145-6, 148
user names 79, 118-19, 148

V

value 2, 21-2, 26, 55, 63, 69, 78, 110, 114, 128, 140
Virtual Private Networks (VPNs) 52, 57, 60
virtualization 40-2, 90, 151, 158-9, 163, 166, 169, 171
volatile 136, 138, 144
VSANs (Virtual SAN) 5, 14, 90-4, 157, 168

W

WWN (World Wide Names) 93, 95, 108, 113, 139

Breinigsville, PA USA
19 August 2010
243819BV00003B/20/P

9 781742 442747